The Closet of Sir Kenelm Digby Knight Opened

Kenelm Digby

A RECEIPT TO MAKE METHEGLIN AS IT IS MADE AT LIEGE, COMMUNICATED BY MR. MASILLON

Take one Measure of Honey, and three Measures of Water, and let it boil till one measure be boiled away, so that there be left three measures in all; as for Example, take to one Pot of Honey, three Pots of Water, and let it boil so long, till it come to three Pots. During which time you must Skim it very well as soon as any scum riseth; which you are to continue till there rise no scum more. You may, if you please, put to it some spice, to wit, Cloves and Ginger; the quantity of which is to be proportioned according as you will have your Meath, strong or weak. But this you do before it begin to boil. There are some that put either Yeast of Beer, or Leaven of bread into it, to make it work. But this is not necessary at all; and much less to set it into the Sun. Mr. Masillon doth neither the one nor the other. Afterwards for to Tun it, you must let it grow Luke-warm, for to advance it. And if you do intend to keep your Meathe a long time, you may put into it some hopps on this fashion. Take to every Barrel of Meathe a Pound of Hops without leaves, that is, of Ordinary Hops used for Beer, but well cleansed, taking only the Flowers, without the Green-leaves and stalks. Boil this pound of Hops in a Pot and half of fair water, till it come to one Pot, and this quantity is sufficient for a Barrel of Meathe. A Barrel at Liege holdeth nincty Pots, and a Pot is as much as a Wine quart in England. (I have since been informed from Liege, that a Pot of that Countrey holdeth 48 Ounces of Apothecary's measure; which I judge to be a Pottle according to London measure, or two Wine-quarts.) When you Tun your Meath, you must not fill your Barrel by half a foot, that so it may have room to work. Then let it stand six weeks slightly stopped; which being expired, if the Meath do not work, stop it up very close. Yet must you not fill up the Barrel to the very brim. After six Months you draw off the clear into another Barrel, or strong Bottles, leaving the dregs, and filling up your new Barrel, or Bottels, and stopping it or them very close.

The Meath that is made this way, (_Viz._ In the Spring, in the Month of April or May, which is the proper time for making of it,) will keep many a year.

WHITE METHEGLIN OF MY LADY HUNGERFORD: WHICH IS EXCEEDINGLY PRAISED

Take your Honey, and mix it with fair water, until the Honey be quite dissolved. If it will bear an Egge to be above the liquor, the breadth of a groat, it is strong enough; if not, put more Honey to it, till it be so strong; Then boil it, till it be clearly and well skimmed; Then put in one good handful of Strawberry-leaves, and half a handful of Violet leaves; and half as much Sorrel: a Douzen tops of Rosemary; four or five tops of Baulme-leaves: a handful of Harts-tongue, and a handful of Liver-worth; a little Thyme, and a little Red-sage; Let it boil about an hour; then put it into a Woodden Vessel, where let it stand, till it be quite cold; Then put it into the Barrel; Then take half an Ounce of Cloves, as much Nutmeg; four or five Races of Ginger; bruise it, and put it into a fine bag, with a stone to make it sink, that it may hang below the middle: Then stop it very close.

The Herbs and Spices are in proportion for six Gallons.

Since my Lady Hungerford sent me this Receipt, she sent me word, that she now useth (and liketh better) to make the Decoction of Herbs before you put the Honey to it, This Proportion of Herbs is to make six Gallons of Decoction, so that you may take eight or nine Gallons of water. When you have drawn out into your water, all the vertue of the Herbs, throw them away, and take the clear Decoction (leaving the settlings) and when it is Lukewarm, Dissolve your proportion of Honey in it. After it is well dissolved and laved with strong Arms or woodden Instruments, like Battle-doors or Scoops, boil it gently; till you have taken away all the scum; then make an end of well boyling it, about an hour in all. Then pour it into a wooden vessel, and let it stand till it be cold. Then pour the clear through a Sieve of hair, ceasing pouring when you come to the foul thick settling. Tun the clear into your vessel (without Barm) and stop it up close, with the Spices in it, till you perceive by the hissing that it begins to work. Then give it some little vent, else the Barrel would break. When it is at the end of the working, stop it up close. She useth to make it at the end of Summer, when she takes up her Honey, and begins to drink it in Lent. But it will be better if you defer piercing it till next Winter. When part of the Barrel is drunk, she botteleth the rest, which maketh it quicker and better. You clear the Decoction from the Herbs by a Hair-sieve.

SOME NOTES ABOUT HONEY

The Honey of dry open Countries, where there is much Wild-thyme, Rosemary, and Flowers, is best. It is of three sorts, Virgin-honey, Life-honey, and Stock-honey. The first is the best. The Life-honey next. The Virgin-honey is of Bees, that swarmed the Spring before, and are taken up in Autumn; and is made best by chusing the Whitest combs of the Hive, and then letting the Honey run out of them lying upon a Sieve without pressing it, or breaking of the Combs. The Life-honey is of the same Combs broken after the Virgin-honey is run from it; The Merchants of Honey do use to mingle all the sorts together. The first of a swarm is called Virgin-honey. That of the next year, after the Swarm was hatched, is Life-honey. And ever after, it is Honey of Old-stocks. Honey that is forced out of the Combs, will always taste of Wax. Hampshire Honey is most esteemed at London. About Bisleter there is excellent good. Some account Norfolk honey the best.

MR. CORSELLISES ANTWERP MEATH

To make good Meath, good white and thick Marsilian or Provence-honey is best; and of that, to four Holland Pints (the Holland Pint is very little bigger then the English Wine-pint:) of Water, you must put two pound of Honey; The Honey must be stirred in Water, till it be all melted; If it be stirred about in warm water, it will melt so much the sooner.

When all is dissolved, it must be so strong that an Egge may swim in it with the end upwards. And if it be too sweet or too strong, because there is too much Honey; then you must put more water to it; yet so, that, as above, an Hens Egge may swim with the point upwards: And then that newly added water must be likewise well stirred about, so that it may be mingled all alike. If the Eggs sink (which is a token that there is not honey enough) then you must put more Honey to it, and stir about, till it be all dissolved, and the Eggs swim, as abovesaid. This being done, it must be hanged over the fire, and as it beginneth to seeth, the scum, that doth arise upon it, both before and after, must be clean skimed off. When it is first set upon the fire, you must measure it first with a stick, how deep the Kettel is, or how much Liquor there be in it; and then it must boil so long, till one third part of it be boiled away. When it is thus boiled, it must be poured out into a Cooler, or open vessel, before it be tunned in the Barrel; but the Bung-hole must be left open, that it may have vent. A vessel, which hath served for Sack is best.

TO MAKE EXCELLENT MEATHE

To every quart of Honey, take four quarts of water. Put your water in a clean Kettle over the fire, and with a stick take the just measure, how high the water cometh, making a notch, where the superficies toucheth the stick. As soon as the water is warm, put in your Honey, and let it boil, skiming it always, till it be very clean; Then put to every Gallon of water, one pound of the best Blew-raisins of the Sun, first clean picked from the stalks, and clean washed. Let them remain in the boiling Liquor, till they be throughly swollen and soft; Then take them out, and put them into a Hair-bag, and strain all the juice and pulp and substance from them in an Apothecaries Press; which put back into your liquor, and let it boil, till it be consumed just to the notch you took at first, for the measure of your water alone. Then let your Liquor run through a Hair-strainer into an empty Woodden-fat, which must stand endwise, with the head of the upper-end out; and there let it remain till the next day, that the liquor be quite cold. Then Tun it up into a good Barrel, not filled quite full, but within three or four fingers breadth; (where Sack hath been, is the best) and let the bung remain open for six weeks with a double bolter-cloth lying upon it, to keep out any foulness from falling in. Then stop it up close, and drink not of it till after nine months.

This Meathe is singularly good for a Consumption, Stone, Gravel, Weak-sight, and many more things. A Chief Burgomaster of Antwerpe, used for many years to drink no other drink but this; at Meals and all times, even for pledging of healths. And though He were an old man, he was of an extraordinary vigor every way, and had every year a Child, had always a great appetite, and good digestion; and yet was not fat.

A WEAKER, BUT VERY PLEASANT, MEATHE

To every quart of Honey take six of water; boil it till 1/3 be consumed, skiming it well all the while. Then pour it into an open Fat, and let it cool. When the heat is well slakened, break into a Bowl-full of this warm Liquor, a New-laid-egge, beating the yolk and white well with it; then put it into the Fat to all the rest of the Liquor, and stir it well together, and it will become very clear. Then pour it into a fit very clean Barrel, and put to it some Mother of Wine, that is in it's best fermentation or working, and this will make the Liquor work also. This will be ready to drink in three or four Months, or sooner.

AN EXCELLENT WHITE MEATHE

Take one Gallon of Honey, and four of water; Boil and scum them till there rise no more scum; then put in your Spice a little bruised, which is most of Cinnamon, a little Ginger, a little Mace, and a very little Cloves. Boil it with the Spice in it, till it bear an Egge. Then take it from the fire, and let it Cool in a Woodden vessel, till it be but lukewarm; which this quantity will be in four or five or six hours. Then put into it a hot tost of White-bread, spread over on both sides, pretty thick with fresh barm; that will make it presently work. Let it work twelve hours, close covered with Cloves. Then Tun it into a Runlet wherein Sack hath been, that is somewhat too big for that quantity of Liquor; for example, that it fill it not by a Gallon; You may then put a little Limon-pill in with it. After it hath remained in the vessel a week or ten days, draw it into Bottles. You may begin to drink it after two or three Months: But it will be better after a year. It will be very spritely and quick and pleasant and pure white.

A RECEIPT TO MAKE A TUN OF METHEGLIN

Take two handfuls of Dock (*alias* wild Carrot) a reasonable burthen of Saxifrage, Wild-sage, Blew-button, Scabious, Bettony, Agrimony, Wild-marjoram, of each a reasonable burthen; Wild-thyme a Peck, Roots and all. All these are to be gathered in the fields, between the two Lady days in Harvest. The Garden-herbs are these; Bay-leaves, and Rosemary, of each two handfuls; a Sieveful of Avens, and as much Violet-leaves: A handful of Sage; three handfuls of Sweet-Marjoram, Three Roots of young Borrage, leaves and all, that hath not born seed; Two handfuls of Parsley-roots, and all that hath not born Seed. Two Roots of Elecampane that have not seeded: Two handfuls of Fennel that hath not seeded: A peck of Thyme; wash and pick all your herbs from filth and grass: Then put your field herbs first into the bottom of a clean Furnace, and lay all your Garden-herbs thereon; then fill your Furnace with clean water, letting your herbs seeth, till they be so tender, that you may easily slip off the skin of your Field-herbs, and that you may break the roots of your Garden-herbs between your Fingers. Then lade forth your Liquor, and set it a cooling. Then fill your Furnace again with clear water to these Herbs, and let them boil a quarter of an hour. Then put it to your first Liquor, filling the Furnace, until you have sufficient to fill your Tun. Then as your Liquor begins to cool, and is almost cold, set your servants to temper Honey and wax in it, Combs and all, and let them temper it well together, breaking the Combes very small; let their hands and nails be very clean; and when you have tempered it very well together, cleanse it through a cleansing sieve into another clean vessel; The more Honey you have in your Liquor, the stronger it will be. Therefore to know, when it is strong enough, take two New-laid eggs, when you begin to cleanse, and put them in whole into the bottom of your cleansed Liquor; And if it be strong enough, it will cause the Egge to ascend upward, and to be on the top as broad as sixpence; if they do not swim on the top; put more.

THE COUNTESS OF BULLINGBROOK'S WHITE METHEGLIN

Take eight Gallons of Conduit-water, and boil it very well; then put as much Honey in it, as will bear an Egge, and stir it well together. Then set it upon the fire, and put in the whites of four Eggs to clarifie it; And as the scum riseth, take it off clean: Then put in a pretty quantity of Rosemary, and let it boil, till it tasteth a little of it: Then with a scummer take out the Rosemary, as fast as you can, and let it boil half a quarter of an hour; put it into earthen pans to cool; next morning put it into a barrel, and put into it a little barm, and an Ounce of Ginger scraped and sliced; And let it stand a Month or six Weeks. Then bottle it up close; you must be sure not to let it stand at all in Brass.

MR. WEBBES MEATH

Master Webbe, who maketh the Kings Meathe, ordereth it thus. Take as much of Hyde-park water as will make a Hogshead of Meathe: Boil in it about two Ounces of the best Hopp's for about half an hour. By that time, the water will have drawn out the strength of the Hopp's. Then skim them clean off, and all the froth, or whatever riseth of the water. Then dissolve in it warm, about one part of Honey to six of water: Lave and beat it, till all the Honey be perfectly dissolved; Then boil it, beginning gently, till all the scum be risen, and scummed away. It must boil in all about two hours. Half an hour, before you end your boiling, put into it some Rosemary-tops, Thyme, Sweet-marjorame, one Sprig of Minth, in all about half a handful, and as much Sweet-bryar-leaves as all these; in all, about a handful of herbs, and two Ounces of sliced Ginger, and one Ounce of bruised Cinamon. He did use to put in a few Cloves and Mace; But the King did not care for them. Let all these boil about half an hour, then scum them clean away; and presently let the Liquor run through a strainer-cloth into a Kiver of wood, to cool and settle. When you see it is very clear and settled, lade out the Liquor into another Kiver, carefully, not to raise the settlings from the bottom. As soon as you see any dregs begin to rise, stay your hand, and let it remain unstirred, till all be settled down. Then lade out the Liquor again, as before; and if need be, change it again into another Kiver: all which is done to the end no dregs may go along with the Liquor in tunning it into the vessel. When it is cold and perfect clear, tun it into a Cask, that hath been used for Sack, and stop it up close, having an eye to give it a little vent, if it should work. If it cast out any foul Liquor in working, fill it up always presently with some of the same liquor, that you have kept in bottles for that end. When it hath wrought, and is well settled (which may be in about two months or ten weeks) draw it into Glass-bottles, as long as it comes clear; and it will be ready to drink in a Month or two: but will keep much longer, if you have occasion: and no dregs will be in the bottom of the bottle.

He since told me, that to this Proportion of Honey and water, to make a Hogshead of Meathe, you should boil half a pound of Hopps in the water, and two good handfuls of Herbs; and six Ounces of Spice of all sorts: All which will be mellowed and rotted away quite, (as well as the lushiousness of the Honey) in the space of a year or two. For this is to be kept so long before it be drunk.

If you would have it sooner ready to drink, you may work it with a little yeast, when it is almost cold in the Kiver: and Tun it up as soon as it begins to work, doing afterwards as is said before; but leaving a little vent to purge by, till it have done working. Or in stead of yeast, you may take the yolks of four New-laid-eggs, and almost half a pint of fine Wheat-flower, and some of the Liquor you have made: beat them well together, then put them to the Liquor in the Cask, and stop it up close, till you see it needful, to give it a little vent.

Note, that yeast of good Beer, is better then that of Ale.

* * * * *

The first of Septemb. 1663. Mr. Webb came to my House to make some for Me. He took fourty three Gallons of water, and fourty two pounds of Norfolk honey. As soon as the water boiled, He put into it a slight handful of Hops; which after it had boiled a little above a quarter of an hour, he skimed off; then put in the honey to the boyling water, and presently a white scum rose, which he skimed off still as it rose; which skiming was ended in little above a quarter of an hour more. Then he put in his herbs and spices, which were these: Rose-mary, Thyme, Winter-savory, Sweet-marjoram, Sweet-bryar-leaves, seven or eight little Parsley-roots: There was most of the Savoury, and least of the Eglantine, three Ounces of Ginger, one Ounce and a half of Cinnamon, five Nutmegs (half an Ounce of Cloves he would have added, but did not,) And these boiled an hour and a quarter longer; in all from the first beginning to boil, somewhat less then two hours: Then he presently laded it out of the Copper into Coolers, letting it run through a Hair-sieve: And set the Coolers shelving (tilted up) that the Liquor might afterwards run the more quietly out of them. After the Liquor had stood so about two hours, he poured or laded out of some of the Coolers very gently, that the dregs might not rise, into other Coolers. And about a pint of very thick dregs remained last in the bottom of every Cooler. That which ran out, was very clear: After two hours more settling, (in a shelving situation,) He poured it out again into other Coolers; and then very little dregs (or scarce any in some of the Coolers) did remain. When the Liquor was even almost cold, He took the yolks of three New-laid-eggs, a spoonful of fine white flower, and about half a pint of new fresh barm of good strong Beer (you must have care that your barm be very white and clean, not sullied and foul, as is usual among slovenly Brewers in London). Beat this very well together, with a little of the Liquor in a skiming dish, till you see it well incorporated, and that it beginneth to work. Then put it to a pailful (of about two Gallons and a half) of the Liquor, and mingle it well therewith. Then leave the skiming dish reversed floating in the middle of the Liquor, and so the yest will work up into and under the hollow of the dish, and grow out round about the sides without. He left this well and thick covered all night, from about eleven a clock at night; And the next morning, finding it had wrought very well, He mingled what was in the Pail with the whole proportion of the Liquor, and so Tunned it up into a Sack-cask. I am not satisfied, whether he did not put a spoonful of fine white good Mustard into his Barm, before he brought it hither, (for he took a pretext to look out some pure clean white barm) but he protested, there was nothing mingled with the barm, yet I am in doubt. He confessed to me that in making of Sider, He put's in half as much Mustard as Barm; but never in Meathe. The fourth of September in the morning, he Bottled up into Quart-bottles the two lesser Rundlets of this Meathe (for he did Tun the whole quantity into one large Rundlet, and two little ones) whereof the one contained thirty Bottles; and the other, twenty two. There remained but little settling or dregs in the Bottom's of the Barrels, but some there was. The Bottles were set into a cool Cellar, and He said they would be ready to drink in three weeks. The Proportion of Herbs and Spices is this; That there be so much as to drown the luscious sweetness of the Honey; but not so much as to taste of herbs or spice, when you drink the Meathe. But that the sweetnes of the honey may kill their taste: And so the Meathe have a pleasant taste, but not of herbs, nor spice, nor honey. And therefore you put more or less according to the time you will drink it in. For a great deal will be mellowed away in a year, that would be ungratefully strong in three months. And the honey that will make it keep a year or two, will require a triple proportion of spice and herbs. He commends Parsley roots to be in greatest quantity, boiled whole, if young; but quarterred and pithed, if great and old.

MY OWN CONSIDERATIONS FOR MAKING OF MEATHE

Boil what quantity of Spring-water you please, three or four walms, and then let it set the twenty four hours, and pour the clear from the settling. Take sixteen Gallons of the clear, and boil in it ten handfuls of Eglantine-leaves, five of Liverwort, five of Scabious, four of Baulm, four of Rosemary; two of Bay-leaves; one of Thyme, and one of Sweet-marjoram, and five Eringo-roots splitted. When the water hath drawn out the vertue of the herbs (which it will do in half an hours boiling,) let it run through a strainer or sieve, and let it settle so, that you may pour the clear from the Dregs. To every three Gallons of the Clear, take one of Honey, and with clean Arms stripped up, lade it for two or three hours, to dissolve the honey in the water; lade it twice or thrice that day. The next day boil it very gently to make the scum rise, and scum it all the while, and now and then pour to it a ladle full of cold water, which will make the scum rise more: when it is very clear from scum, you may boil it the more strongly, till it bear an Egge very high, that the breadth of a groat be out of the water, and that it boil high with great walms in the middle of the Kettle: which boiling with great Bubbles in the middle is a sign it is boiled to it's height. Then let it cool till it be Lukewarm, at which time put some Ale yest into it, to make it work, as you would do Ale. And then put it up into a fit Barrel first seasoned with some good sweet White-wine (as Canary-sack) and keep the bung open, till it have done working, filling it up with some such honey-drink warmed, as you find it sink down by working over. When it hath almost done working, put into it a bag of thin stuff (such as Bakers use to bolt in) fastened by a Cord at the bung, containing two parts of Ginger-sliced, and one apiece of Cinamon, Cloves and Nutmegs, with a Pebble-stone in it to make it sink; And stop it up close for six Months or a year, and then you may draw it into bottles. If you like Cardamon-seeds, you may adde some of them to the spices. Some do like Mint exceedingly to be added to the other herbs. Where no yeast is to be had, The Liquor will work if you set it some days in the hot Sun (with a cover, like the roof of a house over it, to keep wet out, if it chance to rain) but then you must have great care, to fill it up, as it consumeth, and to stop it close a little before it hath done working, and to set it then presently in a Cool Cellar. I am told that the Leaven of bread will make it work as well as yest, but I have not tryed it. If you will not have it so strong, it will be much sooner ready to drink; As if you take six parts of water to one of Honey. Some do like the drink better without either herbs or spices, and it will be much the whiter. If you will have it stronger, put but four Gallons and a half of water to one of honey.

You may use what Herbs or Roots you please, either for their tast or vertue, after the manner here set down.

If you make it work with yeast, you must have great care, to draw it into bottles soon after it hath done working, as after a fortnight or three weeks. For that will make it soon grow stale, and it will thence grow sower and dead before you are aware. But if it work singly of itself, and by help of the Sun without admixtion of either Leaven or Yeast, it may be kept long in the Barrel, so it be filled up to the top, and kept very close stopp'd.

I conceive it will be exceeding good thus: when you have a strong Honey-liquor of three parts of water to one of Honey, well-boiled and scummed, put into it Lukewarm, or better (as soon as you take it from the fire) some Clove-gilly-flowers, first wiped, and all the whites clipped off, one good handful or two to every Gallon of Liquor. Let these infuse 30 or 40 hours. Then strain it from the flowers, and either work it with yeast, or set it in the Sun to work; when it hath almost done working, put into it a bag of like Gilly-flowers (and if they are duly dried, I think they are the better) hanging it in at the bung. And if you will put into it some spirit of wine, that hath drawn a high Tincture from Clove-gilly-flowers (dried I conceive is best) and some other that hath done the like from flowers and tops of Rosemary, and some that hath done the like from Cinnamon and Ginger, I believe it will be much the nobler, and last the longer.

I conceive, that bitter and strong herbs, as Rosemary, Bayes, Sweet-marjoram, Thyme, and the like, do conserve Meathe the better and longer, being as it were in stead of hops. But neither must they, no more than Clove-gilly-flowers, be too much boiled: For the Volatil pure Spirit flies away very quickly. Therefore rather infuse them. Beware of infusing Gillyflower in any vessel of Metal, (excepting silver:) For all Metals will spoil and dead their colour. Glased earth is best.

SACK WITH CLOVE-GILLY FLOWERS

If you will make a Cordial Liquor of Sack with Clove-gilly-flowers, you must do thus. Prepare your Gilly-flowers, as is said before, and put them into great double glass-bottles, that hold two gallons a piece, or more; and put to every gallon of Sack, a good half pound of the wiped and cut flowers, putting in the flowers first, and then the Sack upon them. Stop the glasses exceeding close, and set them in a temperate Cellar. Let them stand so, till you see that the Sack hath drawn out all the principal tincture from them, and that the flowers begin to look palish; (with an eye of pale, or faint in Colour) Then pour the Sack from them, and throw away the exhausted flowers, or distil a spirit from them; For if you let them remain longer in the Sack, they will give an earthy tast to them. You may then put the tincted Sack into fit bottles for your use, stopping them very close. But if the season of the flowers be not yet past, your Sack will be better, if you put it upon new flowers, which I conceive will not be the worse, but peradventure the better, if they be a little dried in the shade. If you drink a Glass or two of this sack at a meal, you will find it a great Cordial.

Upon better consideration; I conceive the best way of making Hydromel with Clove-gilly-flowers, is thus: Boil your simple Liquor to its full height (with three parts of water to one of Honey), take a small parcel out, to make a strong infusion of flowers, pouring it boyling hot upon the flowers in earthen vessels. If you have great quantity, as six to one, of Liquor, you will easily draw out the tincture in fourteen or sixteen hours infusion; otherwise you may quicken your liquor with a parcel of Sack. In the mean time make the great quantity of Liquor work with yest. When it hath almost done fermenting, but not quite, put the infusion to it warm, and let it ferment more if it will. When that is almost done, put to it a bag with flowers to hang in the bung.

I conceive that Hydromel made with Juniper-berries (first broken and bruised) boiled in it, is very good. Adde also to it Rosemary and Bay-leaves.

Upon tryal of several ways, I conclude (as things yet appear to me) that to keep Meath long, it must not be fermented with yest (unless you put Hops to it) but put it in the barrel, and let it ferment of it self, keeping a thick plate of lead upon the bung, to lie close upon it, yet so that the working of the Liquor may raise it, to purge out the foulness, and have always some new made plain Liquor, to fill it up as it sinks, warm whiles it works: but cold during three or four month's after. Then stop the bung exceeding close. And when you will make your Mead with Cherries or Morello-Cherries, or Raspes, or Bilberries, or Black-cherries, put their juyce to the Liquor when you tun it, without ever boiling it therein; about one quart of juyce to every three or four gallons of Liquor. You may squeese out the clear juyce, and mingle it with the Liquor, and hang the Magma in a bag in the bung. I think it is best to break the stones of the Cherries, before you put their Magma into the bag.

Since I conceive, that Clove-gilly-flowers must never be boiled in the Liquor: that evaporateth their Spirits, which are very volatile: But make a strong infusion of them, and besides hang a Bag of them in the bung. I conceive that it is good to make the Liquor pretty strong (not too much, but so as the taste may be gratefull) of some strong herbs, as Rosemary, Bay-leaves, Sweet-marjoram, Thyme, Broad-thyme, and the like. For they preserve the drink, and make it better for the stomack and head. Standing in the Sun is the best way of Fermentation, when the drink is strong. The root of Angelica or Elecampane, or Eringo, or Orris, may be good and pleasant, to be boiled in the Liquor. Raspes and Cherries and Bilberies are never to be boiled, but their juyce put into the Liquor, when it is tunning. Use onely Morello-Cherries (I think) for pleasure, and black ones for health. I conceive it best to use very little spice of any kind in Meathes.

METHEGLIN COMPOSED BY MY SELF OUT OF SUNDRY RECEIPTS

In sixty Gallons of water, boil ten handfuls of Sweet-bryar-leaves; Eye-bright, Liverwort, Agrimony, Scabious, Balme, Wood-bettony, Strawberry-leaves, Burnet, of each four handfuls; of Rosemary, three handfuls; of Minth, Angelica, Bayes and Wild-thyme, Sweet-Marjoram, of each two handfuls: Six Eringo-roots. When the water hath taken out the vertue of the herbs and roots, let it settle, and the next day pour off the clear, and in every three Gallons of it boil one of honey, scumming it well, and putting in a little cold water now and then to make the scum rise, as also some whites of Eggs. When it is clear scummed, take it *off*, and let it cool; then work it with Ale-yest; tun it up, and hang it in a bag, with Ginger, Cinamom, Cloves and Cardamom. And as it worketh over, put in some strong honey-drink warmed. When it works no more, stop it up close.

In twenty Gallons of water boil Sweet-bryar-leaves, Eye-bright, Rosemary, Bayes, Clove-gilly-flowers of each five handfuls, and four Eringo-roots. To every two gallons and a half of this decoction, put one gallon of honey; boil it, &c. When it is tunned up, hang in it a bag containing five handfuls of Clove-gilly-flowers, and sufficient quantity of the spices above.

In both these Receipts, the quantity of the herbs is too great. The strong herbs preserve the drink, and make it nobler. Use Marjoram and Thyme in little quantity in all.

MY LADY COWERS WHITE MEATHE USED AT SALISBURY

Take to four Gallons of water, one Gallon of Virgin-honey; let the water be warm before you put in the honey; and then put in the whites of 3 or 4 Eggs well beaten, to make the scum rise. When the honey is throughly melted and ready to boil, put in an Egge with the shell softly; and when the Egge riseth above the water, to the bigness of a groat in sight, it is strong enough of the honey. The Egge will quickly be hard, and so will not rise; Therefore you must put in another, if the first do not rise to your sight; you must put in more water and honey proportionable to the first, because of wasting away in the boiling. It must boil near an hour. You may, if you please, boil in it, a little bundle of Rosemary, Sweet-marjoram, and Thyme; and when it tasteth to your liking, take it forth again. Many do put Sweet-bryar berries in it, which is held very good. When your Meath is boiled enough take it off the fire, and put it into a Kiver; when it is blood-warm, put in some Ale-barm, to make it work, and cover it close with a blancket in the working. The next morning tun it up, and if you please put in a bag with a little Ginger and a little Nutmeg bruised; and when it hath done working, stop it up close for a Moneth, and then Bottle it.

SIR THOMAS GOWER'S METHEGLIN FOR HEALTH

First boil the water and scum it; Then to 12 Gallons put 6 handfuls of Sweet-bryar-leaves, of Sweet-marjoram, Rosemary, Thyme, of each one a handful: Flowers of Marigold, Borrage, Bugloss, Sage, each two handfuls. Boil all together very gently, till a third waste. To eight Gallons of this put two Gallons of pure honey, and boil them till the Liquor bear an Egge, the breadth of threepence or a Groat, together with such spices as you like (bruised, but not beaten) an ounce of all is sufficient.

You must observe carefully. 1. Before you set the Liquor to boil, to cause a lusty Servant (his Arms well washed) to mix the honey and water together, labouring it with his hands at least an hour without intermission. 2. That when it begins to boil fast, you take away part of the fire, so as it may boil slowly, and the scum and dross go all to one side, the other remaining clear. When you take it off, let none of the liquor go away with the dross. 3. When you take it from the fire, let it settle well, before it be tunned into the vessel, wherein you mean to keep it: and when it comes near the bottom, let it be taken carefully from the sediment, with a thin Dish, so as nothing be put into the vessel, but what is clear. 4. Stop it very close (when it is set in the place, where it must remain) cover it with a cloth, upon which some handfuls of Bay-salt and Salpeter is laid, and over that lay clay, and a Turf. 5. Put into it, when you stop it, some New-laid-eggs in number proportionable to the bigness of the vessel, Shell's unbroken. Six Eggs to about sixteen Gallons. The whole Egg-shell and all will be entirely consumed.

METHEGLIN FOR TASTE AND COLOUR

Must be boiled as the other, if you intend to keep it above half a year; but less according to the time, wherein you mean to use it. You must put in no Herbs, to avoid bitterness and discolouring; and the proportion of water and honey more or less, as you would drink it sooner or later; (as a Gallon of honey to 4, 5, or 6 of water.) If to be weak, and to be soon drunk, you must when it is tunned, put in a Tost of bread (hard tosted) upon which half a score drops of Spirit of yest or barm is dropped; for want of it, spread it with purest barm beaten with a few drops of Oyl of Cinnamon. If you intend to give it the taste of

Raspes, then adde more barm, to make it work well, and during that time of working, put in your Raspes (or their Syrup) but the fruit gives a delicate Colour, and Syrup a duller Tincture. Drink not that made after the first manner, till six moneths, and it will endure drawing better then wine; but Bottleled, it is more spirited then any drink.

The Spirit of Barm is made by putting store of water to the barm; then distill the Spirit, as you do other Spirits; At last an oyl will come, which is not for this use.

Sir Thomas Gower maketh his ordinary drink thus: Make very small well Brewed Ale. To eight Gallons of this put one Gallon of honey; when it is well dissolved and clarified, tun up the Liquor, making it work in due manner with barm. When it hath done working, stop it up close, and in three months it will be fit to drink.

He makes Metheglin thus. Make a good Decoct of Eglantine-leaves, Cowslip flowers, a little Sweet-marjoram, and some Rosemary and Bay-leaves, Betony, and Scabious, and a little Thyme. After the sediment hath settled, put 1/3 or 1/4 or 1/5 or 1/6 part of honey, (according as you would have it strong, and soon ready) to the clear severed from the settlement, and stir it exceeding well with stripped arms 4 or 5 hours, till it be perfectly incorporated. Then boil and scum it; let it then cool and tun it up, &c. After it hath cooled, lade the clean from the settlement, so that it may not trouble it, and run up the clear thus severed from the settlings. Much of the perfection consisteth in stirring it long with stripped arms before you boil it. Then to boil it very leisurely till all the scum be off. And order your fire so, that the scum may rise and drive all to one side. This will be exceeding pale clear and pleasant Metheglin. He useth to every Gallon of water, a good handful of Eglantine-leaves, and as much Cowslip flowers; but onely a Pugil of Thyme or Marjoram.

AN EXCELLENT WAY OF MAKING WHITE METHEGLIN

Take of Sweet-bryar berries, of Rosemary, broad Thyme, of each a handful. Boil them in a quantity of fair water for half an hour; then cleanse the water from the herbs, and let it stand 24 hours, until it be thorough cold. Then put your hony into it (hony which floweth from the Combs of it self in a warm place is best) make it so strong of the honey that it bear an egge (if you will have it strong) the breadth of a groat above the Liquor. This being done, lave and bounce it very well and often, that the honey and water may incorporate and work well together. After this boil it softly over a gentle fire, and scum it. Then beat the whites of eggs with their shells, and put into it to clarifie it. After this, put some of it into a vessel, and take the whites of two eggs, and a little barm, and a small quantity of fine flower; beat them well together, and put it into the vessel close covered, that it may work. Then pour the rest into it by degrees, as you do Beer. At last take a quantity of Cinamon, 2 or 3 races of Ginger, and two Nutmegs (for more will alter the colour of it.) Hang these in a little bag in the vessel. Thus made, it will be as white as any White-wine.

ANOTHER WAY OF MAKING WHITE METHEGLIN

To three Gallons of Spring-water take three quarts of honey, and set it over the fire, till the scum rises pretty thick. Then take off the scum, and put in Thyme, Rosemary, Hyssop and Maiden-hair, of each one handful; and two handfuls of Eglantine leaves, and half a handful of Organ. The spices, Ginger, Nutmegs, Cinamon and a little mace, and boil all these together near half an hour. Then take it from the fire, and let it stand till it be cold, and then strain it, and so Tun it up, and stop it close. The longer you keep it, the better it will be.

ANOTHER WAY

Take two Gallons of water; one Gallon of Honey: Parietary one handful; Sage, Thyme, one Pugil; Of Hyssop half a Pugil. Six Parsley-roots; one Fennel-root, the pith taken out: Red-nettles one Pugil. Six leaves of Hearts-tongue. Boil this together one hour. Then put in the Honey, and Nutmegs, Cloves, Mace, Cinamon of each one ounce; of Ginger three ounces. Boil all these together, till the scum be boiled in, not scumming it. Then take it off, and set it to cool. When it is cold, put in it six spoonfuls of barm, and when it is ripe, it will hiss in the pail. You must take out the herbs, when you put in the honey. If you put in these herbs following, it will be far better; Sanicle, Bugloss, Avens, and

Ladies-mantle, of each one handful.

TO MAKE WHITE METHEGLIN

Take of Sweet-bryar a great handful: of Violet-flowers, Sweet-marjoram, Strawberry-leaves, Violet-leaves, *ana*, one handful, Agrimony, Bugloss, Borrage, *ana*, half a handful. Rosemary four branches, Gilly-flowers, No. 4 (the Yellow-wall-flowers, with great tops) Anniseeds, Fennel, and Caraway, of each a spoonful, Two large Mace. Boil all these in twelve Gallons of water for the Space of an hour; then strain it, and let it stand until it be Milk-warm Then put in as much honey, as will carry an Egge to the breadth of sixpence, at least. Then boil it again, and scum it clean; then let it stand, until it be cold; then put a pint of Ale-barm into it, and ripen it as you do Beer, and tun it. Then hang in the midst of the vessel a little bag with a Nutmeg quartered, a Race of Ginger sliced, a little Cinamon, and mace whole, and three grains of Musk in a cloth put into the bag amongst the rest of the Spices. Put a stone in the bag, to keep it in the midst of the Liquor. This quantity took up three Gallons of honey; therefore be sure to have four in readiness.

STRONG MEAD

Take one Measure of honey, and dissolve it in four of water, beating it long up and down with clean Woodden ladels. The next day boil it gently, scumming it all the while till no more scum riseth; and if you will clarifie the Liquor with a few beaten whites of Eggs, it will be the clearer. The rule of it's being boiled enough is, when it yieldeth no more scum, and beareth an Egge, so that the breadth of a groat is out of the water. Then pour it out of the Kettle into woodden vessels, and let it remain there till it be almost cold. Then Tun it into a vessel, where Sack hath been.

A RECEIPT FOR MAKING OF MEATH

Take a quart of honey, and mix it with a Gallon of Fountain-water, and work it well four days together, four times a day; The fifth day put it over the fire, and let it boil an hour, and scum it well. Then take the whites of two Eggs, and beat them to a froth, and put it into the Liquor; stirring it well, till the whites of Eggs have raised a froth of Scum; then take it off, scumming the liquor clean. Then take a handful of Strawberry-leaves and Violet-leaves together, with a little Sprig of Rosemary and two or three little Sprigs of Spike; and so boil it again (with these herbs in it) a quarter of an hour. Then take it off the fire, and when it is cold, put it into a little barrel, and put into it half a spoonful of Ale-yest, and let it work; which done, take one Nutmeg sliced, and twice as much Ginger sliced, six Cloves bruised, and a little stick of Cinamon, and sow these Spices in a little bag, and stop it well; and it will be fit for use within a fortnight, and will last half a year. If you will have your Metheglin stronger, put into it a greater quantity of honey.

MY LORD HOLLIS HYDROMEL

In four parts of Springwater dissolve one part of honey, or so much as the Liquor will bear an Egge to the breadth of a Groat. Then boil it very well, and that all the scum be taken away. He addeth nothing to it but a small proportion of Ginger sliced: of which He putteth half to boil in the Liquor, after all the scum is gone; and the other half He putteth into a bag, and hangeth in the bung, when it is tunned. The Ginger must be very little, not so much as to make the Liquor taste strongly of it, but to quicken it. I should like to adde a little proportion of Rosemary, and a greater of Sweet-bryar leaves, in the boiling. As also, to put into the barrel a tost of white bread with mustard, to make it work. He puts nothing to it; but his own strength in time makes it work of it self. It is good to drink after a year.

A RECEIPT FOR WHITE METHEGLIN

Take to every quart of honey, 4, 5, or 6, quarts of water; boil it on a good quick fire as long as any scum riseth; as it boils, put about half a pint of water at a time very often, and scum it very well as it riseth; and be sure to keep it up to the same height and quantity as at the first: Put into it a little Rosemary, according to the quantity that you make, and boil it half a quarter of an hour; scum it very well. You may put a little Ginger into it, onely to give it a taste thereof, and let it have a little walm of heat after it. Then take and put it into a Woodden vessel, (which must be well scalded, least it taste of any thing) let it stand all night, and the next morning strain it through a sieve of hair.

Then if you please, you may boil up your grounds that are in the bottome of the vessel with three or four quarts of water; and when it is cold, strain it, to the rest, and put to it a little good light barm. That which you make in the winter, you must let it stand three days and three nights covered up, before you bottle it up; and two nights in summer, and then bottle it up. But be sure, you scum off the barm before the bottling up.

Your Vessel, which you intend to boil your Meath in, must stand in scalding water, whilst you boil your Meath; it will drink up the less of your Meath. Four spoonfuls of good new Ale-barm will serve for five quarts of honey. As you desire your Metheglin in strength, so take at the first either of the quantities of water. Five quarts is reasonable.

HYDROMEL AS I MADE IT WEAK FOR THE QUEEN MOTHER

Take 18 quarts of spring-water, and one quart of honey; when the water is warm, put the honey into it. When it boileth up, skim it very well, and continue skimming it, as long as any scum will rise. Then put in one Race of Ginger (sliced in thin slices,) four Cloves, and a little sprig of green Rosemary. Let these boil in the Liquor so long, till in all it have boiled one hour. Then set it to cool, till it be blood-warm; and then put to it a spoonful of Ale-yest. When it is worked up, put it into a vessel of a fit size; and after two or three days, bottle it up. You may drink it after six weeks, or two moneths.

Thus was the Hydromel made that I gave the Queen, which was exceedingly liked by everybody.

SEVERAL WAYS OF MAKING METHEGLIN

Take such quantity as you judge convenient of Spring, or pure rain water, and make it boil well half an hour. Then pour it out into a Woodden fat, and let it settle 74 hours. Then power off the clear, leaving the sediment in the bottome. Let such water be the Liquor for all the several Honey-drinks, you will make.

1. Warm sixteen Gallons of this water (lukewarm) and put two Gallons of Honey to it, in a half tub or other fit Woodden vessel. Lave it very well with a clean arm, or woodden battle-door for two or three hours, dissolving the honey very well in the water. Let it stand thus two or three days in wood, laving it thrice a day, a pretty while each time. Then put it back into your Copper and boil it gently, till you have scummed away all the foulness that will rise; and clarifie it with whites of Eggs: Then put into it a little handful of cleansed and sliced white Ginger, and a little mace; when they have boiled enough, put in a few Cloves bruised, and a stick of Cinamon, and a little Limmon-peel, and after a walm or two, pour the Liquor into a woodden half tub, with the spices in it. Cover it close with a Cloth and blanquet, and let it stand so two days. Then let the liquor run through a bolter, to sever the spice, stopping before any settlings come. Then pour this clear liquor into pottle-bottles of glass, not filling them by a fingers breadth or more. Stop them close with Cork tied in, and set them in a cool place for 6, 7 or 8 weeks.

2. In fourty Gallons of the first boiled and settled water, boil five handfuls of sweet-bryar tops, as much of Cowslip-flowers, as much of Primrose-flowers, as much of Rosemary-flowers, as much of Sage-flowers, as many of Borage-flowers, as many of Bugloss-flowers; two handfuls of the tops of Betony, four handfuls of Agrimony, and as many of Scabious, one handful of Thyme, as much of Sweet-marjoram, and two ounces of Mustard-seed bruised. When this hath boiled so long, that you judge the water hath drawn out all the vertue of the Herbs (which may be in half an hour) pour out all into a vatte to cool and settle. Scum away the herbs, and pour the clear from the sediment, and to every four gallons of liquor (luke-warm) put one gallon of honey, and lave it to dissolve the honey, letting it stand two or three days, laving it well thrice every day. Then boil it till it will bear an Egge high, then clarifie it with whites and shells of Eggs, and pour it into a vatte to cool, which it will do in a days space or better. Whilst it is yet luke-warm, put Ale-yest to it, (no more then is necessary) to make it

work, and then tun it into a Rundlet of a fit Size, that hath been seasoned with Sack; and hang in it a boulter bag containing half a pound of white Ginger cleansed and sliced, three ounces of Cloves and as much of Cinamon bruised, as much Coriander seed prepared, and as much Elder-flowers. As it purgeth and consumeth by running over the bung, put in fresh honey-liquor warmed, that you keep or make on purpose for that end. When the working is even almost at an end, stop it up close with clay and sand, and have great care to keep it always close stopped. After a year draw in into pottle Glass-bottles stopped with ground stoppels of glass, and keep them in a cool place, till they are ready to drink, if they as yet be not so.

Have a care, that never any Liquor stay in Copper longer then whilst it is to boil.

3. In 20 Gallons of the first boiled and settled water, boil six handfuls of Sweet-bryar-leaves, as many of Cowslip flowers, as many of Primrose-flowers, and as many of Rosemary-flowers; and half a handful of Wild thyme, during the space of a quarter or half an hour. Then take the clear, and dissolve in it a sixth part of honey, doing as above for the boiling and clarifying it. But boil it not to bear an Egge, but onely till it be well scummed and clarified. Then pour it into a woodden Tub, and Tun it with Ale-yest, when it is in due temper of coolness, as you would do Ale-wort; and let it work (close covered) sufficiently. Then Tun it up into a seasoned firkin, and put into it a tost of white-bread spread with quick Mustard, and hang it in a boulter bag containing loosly some Ginger, Cloves and Cinamon bruised, and a little Limon-peel and Elder-flowers, with a Pebble-stone at the bottome, to make it sink towards the bottom, and fastned by a string coming out of the bung to hinder it from falling quite to the bottome. Stop the bung very close, and after six weeks or two moneths draw it into bottles.

4. In 20 Gallons of boiled and settled water, boil a quarter of an hour ten handfuls of sweet bryar-leaves, and as many of Cowslips. Then let it cool and settle in wood, and take the clear; and to every four Gallons of Liquor, put one of honey, dissolving it as the others formerly set down. Boil it, till no more scum rise, and that a fourth part be

consumed. Then clarifie it with whites of Eggs and their shells, and make it work with yest. After sufficient working Tun it up, hanging it in a bag with Ginger, Cloves, Cinamon and Limon-peel. Stop it very close, and after two or three moneths, draw it into bottles.

MY LADY MORICES MEATH

Boil first your water with your herbs. Those she likes best, are, Angelica, Balm, Borage, and a little Rosemary (not half so much as of any of the rest) a handful of all together, to two or 3 Gallons of water. After about half an hours boiling, let the water run through a strainer (to sever the herbs from it) into Woodden or earthen vessels, and let it cool and settle. To three parts of the clear, put one or more of honey, and boil it till it bear an Egge, leaving as broad as a shilling out of the water, skiming it very well. Then power it out into vessels, as before; and next day, when it is almost quite cold, power it into a Sack-cask, wherein you have first put a little fresh Ale-yest, about two spoonfuls to ten Gallons. Hang it in a bag with a little sliced Ginger, but almost a Porengerfull of Cloves. Cover the bung lightly, till it have done working; then stop it up close. You may tap and draw it a year or two after. It is excellent good.

MY LADY MORICE HER SISTER MAKES HER'S THUS:

Dissolve your honey in the water till it bear an Egge higher or lower, according to the strength you will have it of. Then put into it some Sea-wormwood and a little Rosemary, and a little Sage; about too good handfuls of all together, to ten Gallons. When it hath boiled enough to take the vertue of the herbs, skim them out, and strew a handful or two of fine Wheat-flower upon the boyling Liquor.

This will draw all the dregs to it, and swim at the top, so that you may skim all off together. And this she holdeth the best way of clarifying the Liquor, and making it look pale. Then pour it into vessels as above to cool. Let it stand three days; then Tun it up into a Sack cask without yest or Spice, and keep it stopped till it work. Then let it be open, till it have done working, filling it up still with other honey-drink. Then stop it up close for a year or two. You may at first stop it so, that the strong working may throw out the stopple, and yet keep it close, till it work strongly. She saith, that such a small proportion of wormwood giveth it a fine quick tast, and a pale colour with an eye of green. The wormwood must not be so much, as to discern any the least bitterness in the taste; but that the composition of it with the honey may give a quickness. The Rosemary and Sage must be a great deal less then the Wormwood. Sometimes she stoppeth it up close as soon as she hath Tunned it, and lets it remain so for three moneths. Then pierce it and draw it into bottles, which stop well, and tie down the stoppels. This will keep so a long time. She useth this way most. It makes the Mead drink exceeding quick and pleasant. When you pierce the Cask, it will flie out with exceeding force, and be ready to throw out the stopper and spigot.

TO MAKE WHITE MEATH

Take Rosemary, Thyme, Sweet-bryar, Penyroyal, Bayes, of each one handful; steep them 24 hours in a bowl of fair cold water covered close; next day boil them very well in another water, till the colour be very high; then take another water, and boil the same herbs in it, till it look green; and so boil them in several waters, till they do but just change the colour of the water. The first waters are thrown away. The last water must stand 24 hours with the herbs in it. The Liquor being strained from them, you must put in as much fine honey till it will bear an Egge; you must work and labour the honey with the Liquor a whole day, till the honey be consumed; then let it stand a night a clearing. In the morning put your Liquor a boiling for a quarter of an hour, with the whites and shells of six Eggs. So strain it through a bag, and let it stand a day a cooling; so Tun it up, and put into the vessel in a Linnen bag, Cloves, Mace, Cinamon and Nutmegs bruised altogether. If you will have it to drink presently, take the whites of two or three Eggs, of barm a spoonful, and as much of Wheaten-flower. Then let it work before you stop it, afterwards stop it well with Clay and Salt. A quart of Honey to a Gallon of liquor, and so proportionably for these Herbs.

SIR WILLIAM PASTON'S MEATHE

Take ten Gallons of Spring-water, and put therein ten Pints of the best honey. Let this boil half an hour, and scum it very well; then put in one handful of Rosemary, and as much of Bay-leaves; with a little Limon-peel. Boil this half an hour longer, then take it off the fire, and put it into a clean Tub; and when it is cool, work it up with yest, as you do Beer. When it is wrought, put it into your vessel, and stop it very close. Within three days you may Bottle it, and in ten days after it will be fit to drink.

ANOTHER PLEASANT MEATHE OF SIR WILLIAM PASTON'S

To a Gallon of water put a quart of honey, about ten sprigs of Sweet-Majoram; half so many tops of Bays. Boil these very well together, and when it is cold, bottle it up. It will be ten days before it be ready to drink.

ANOTHER WAY OF MAKING MEATH

Boil Sweet Bryar, Sweet Marjoram, Cloves and Mace in Spring-water, till the water taste of them. To four Gallons of water put one Gallon of honey, and boil it a little to skim and clarifie it. When you are ready to take it from the fire, put in a little Limon-peel, and pour it into a Woodden vessel, and let it stand till it is almost cold. Then put in some Ale-yest, and stir it altogether. So let it stand till next day. Then put a few stoned Raisins of the Sun into every bottle, and pour the Meath upon them. Stop the bottles close, and in a week the Meath will be ready to drink.

SIR BAYNAM THROCKMORTON'S MEATHE.

Take four quarts of Honey, good measure; put to it four Gallons of water, let it stand all night, but stir it well, when you put it together. The next day boil it, and put to it Nutmegs, Cloves, Mace and Ginger, of each half an ounce. Let these boil with the honey and water till it will bear an Egge at the top without sinking; and then it is enough, if you see the Egge the breadth of a sixpence. The next day put it in your vessel, and put thereto two or three spoonfuls of barm; and when it hath done working, you may (if you like it) put in a little Ambergreece in a clout with a stone to it to make it sink. This should be kept a whole year before it be drunk; it will drink much the better, free from any tast of the honey, and then it will look as clear as Sack. Make it not till Michaelmas, and set it in a cool place. You may drink it a quarter old, but it will not taste so pleasant then, as when it is old.

TO MAKE WHITE METHEGLIN

Take a Gallon of Honey; put to it four Gallons of water; stir them well together, and boil them in a Kettle, till a Gallon be wasted with boiling and scumming. Then put it into a vessel to cool. When it is almost as cold as Ale-wort, then clear it out into another vessel: Then put Barm upon it, as you do to your Ale, and so let it work. And then Tun it up into a vessel, and put into it a bag with Ginger, Cloves, and Cinamon bruised a little, and so hang the bag in the vessel, and stop it up very close; and when it hath stood a month or six weeks, bottle it up and so drink it. You may put in a little Limmon-peel into some of your Metheglin, for those that like that taste; which most persons do very much.

A RECEIPT FOR MAKING OF MEATH

Mistress Hebden telleth me, that the way of making Honey-drink in Russia, is thus; Take for example, 100 Gallons of Spring water, boil it a little; then let it stand 24 hours to cool, and much sediment will fall to the bottom; from which pour the clear, and warm it, and put 20 or 25 Gallons of pure honey to it, and lade it a long time with a great woodden battle-dore, till it be well dissolved. The next day boil it gently, till you have skimed off all the scum that will rise, and that it beareth an Egge boyant. And in this Liquor you must put, in the due time, a little quantity of Hops, about two handfuls, which must boil sufficiently in the Liquor. Put this into the cooling fat to cool two or three days. When it is about milk-warm, take white-bread and cut it into tosts, upon which, (when they are hot) spread moderately thick some fresh sweet Ale-yest; and cover the superficies of the Liquor with such tosts; Then cover the Tub or Fat with a double course sheet, and a blancket or two, which tye fast about it. This will make your Liquor work up highly. When you find it is near it's height of working, and that the Liquor is risen to the top of the Tub (of which it wanted 8 or 10

Inches at first,) Skim off the tosts and yest, and Tun it up in a hogshead: which stop close; but after 24 hours draw it into another barrel: for it will leave a great deal of sediment. It will work again in this second barrel. After other 24 hours draw it into another barrel, and then it will be clear and pale like White-wine. Stop it up close, hanging a bag of bruised spice in the bung; and after five or six months, it will be fit to drink. If you would have your Meath taste of Raspes, or Cherries (Morello, sharp Cherries, are the best) prepare the water first with them; by putting five or six Gallons of either of these fruits, or more, into this proportion of water; in which bruise them to have all their juyce: but strain the Liquor from the Grains or Seeds, or Stones. And then proceed with this tincted water, as is said above. You may make your Liquor as strong, as you like, of the fruit. Cardamon-seeds mingled with the suspended spices, adde much to the pleasantness of the drink. Limon-peel, as also Elder-flowers.

MY LADY BELLASSISES MEATH

The way of making is thus. She boileth the honey with Spring-water, as I do, till it be cleer scumed; then to every Gallon of Honey, put in a pound or two of good Raisins of the Sun; boil them well, and till the Liquor bear an Egge. Then pour it into a Cowl or Tub to cool. In about 24 hours it will be cool enough to put the yest to it, being onely Lukewarm: which do thus: spread yest upon a large hot tost, and lay it upon the top of the Liquor, and cover the Tub well, first with a sheet, then with coverlets, that it may work well. When it is wrought up to it's height, before it begin to sink, put it into your barrel, letting it run through a loose open strainer, to sever the Raisins and dregs from it. Stop it up close, and after it hath been thus eight or ten days, draw it into bottles, and into every bottle put a cod of Cardamoms, having first a little bruised them as they lie in the cod; and opening the cod a little, that the Liquor may search into it. Stop your bottles close, and after three or four moneths you may drink, and it will be very pleasant and quick, and look like white wine.

ANOTHER METHEGLIN

In every three Gallons of water, boil Rosemary, Liverwort, Balm, *ana*, half a handful, and Cowslips two handfuls. When the water hath sufficiently drawn out the vertue of the herbs, pour all into a Tub, and let it stand all night. Then strain it. And to every three Gallons of the clear Liquor (or 2-1/2, if you will have your drink stronger) put one Gallon of honey, and boil it, till it bear an Egge, scuming it till no more scum will rise: which to make rise the better, put in now and then a Porrenger full of cold water. Then pour it into a Tub, and let it stand to cool, till it be blood warm, and then put by degrees a Pint of Ale-yest to it, to make it work. So let it stand three days very close covered. Then skim off the yest, and put it into a seasoned barrel; but stop it not up close, till it have done hissing. Then either stop it very close, if you will keep it in the barrel, or draw it into bottles. Put into this proportion, Ginger sliced, Nutmegs broken, *ana*, one ounce, Cinamon bruised half an ounce in a bag, which hang in the bung with a stone in it to make it sink. You may add, if you please, to this proportion of water, or one Gallon more, two handfuls of Sweet-bryar-leaves, and one of Betony.

MR. PIERCE'S EXCELLENT WHITE METHEGLIN

In a Copper, that holdeth conveniently three hogsheads, or near so much, boil the best water, (as full as is fitting). As soon as it boileth well and high, put to it four handfuls of Sweet-bryar-leaves, as much of Eye-bright: two handfuls of Rosemary, as much of Sweet-Marjoram, and one of Broad-thyme. Let them boil a quarter of an hour (He letteth them boil no longer, to preserve the colour of the Metheglin pale) then scum away the herbs, scuming also the water clear. Then lade out the water, (letting it run through a Ranch-Sieve) into a wide open vessel, or large Vat to cool, leaving the settlement and dregs. (He often leaves out the Eye-bright and Thyme, when he provideth chiefly for the pure tast; though the Eye-bright hurts it but little.) When it is blood-warm, put the honey to it, about one part, to four of water; but because this doth not determine the proportions exactly (for some honey will make it stronger then other) you must do that by bearing up an Egge. But first, lave and scoop your mixture exceedingly, (at least an hour) that the honey be not onely perfectly dissolved, but uniformly mixed throughout the water. Then take out some of it in a great Woodden bowl or pail, and put a good number, (ten or twelve) New-laid-eggs into it, and as round ones as may be; For long ones will deceive you in the swiming; and stale ones, being lighter then new, will emerge out of the Liquor, the breadth of a sixpence, when new ones will not a groats-breadth. Therefore you take many, that you make a medium of their several emergings; unless you be certain, that they which you use, are immediately then laid and very round. The rule is, that a Groats-breadth (or rather but a threepence) of the Egg-shel must Swim above the Liquor; which then put again into your Copper to boil. It will be some while, before it boil, (peradventure a goodquarter of an hour) but all that while scum will rise, which skim away still as it riseth; and it should be clear scummed by then it boileth: which as soon as it doth, turn up an hour Glass, and let it boil well a good hour. A good quarter before the hour is out, put to it a pound of White-Ginger beaten exceedingly small and searsed (which will sever all the skins and course parts from the fine) which having boiled a quarter of an hour, so to make up the whole hour of boiling, pour out the Liquor into wide open Vats to cool. When it is quite cold, put a pottle of New-ale-barm into a Pipe or Butt, standing endwise with his head out, and pour upon it a Pail-full of your cool Liquor out of one of the Vats; which falling from high upon it with force, will break and dissipate the barm into atoms, and mix it with the Liquor. Pour immediately another pail-ful to that, continuing to do so, till all the Liquor be in. Which by this time and this course will be uniformly mixed with the barm, and begin to work. Yet scoop and lade it well a while, to make the mixtion more perfect, and set the working well on foot. Then cover your But-head with a sheet onely in Summer, but blankets in Winter; and let your Liquor work about 24 hours or more. The measure of that is, till the barm (which is raised to a great head) beginneth a little to fall. Then presently scum of the thick head of the barm, but take not all away so scrupulously, but that there may remain a little white froth upon the face of the Liquor. Which scoop and lade strongly, mingling all to the bottom, that this little remaining barm may by this agitation be mixed a new with the whole. Then immediately Tun this Liquor into two hogsheads that have served for Spanish-wine (be sure to fill them quite full) and there let it work two or three days; that is to say, till you see that all the feculent substance is wrought out, and that what runneth out, beginneth to be clear, though a little whitish or frothy on the upperside of the stream that runs down along the outside of the hogshead. (If there should be a little more then to fill two hogsheads, put it in a Rundlet by it self.) Then take some very strong firm Paper, and wet it on one side with some of the barm that works out, and lay that side over the bung to cover it close. The barm will make it stick fast to the hogshead. This covering will serve for a moneth or two. Then stop it close with strong Cork fitted to the hole, with a linnen about it, to press it fast in: But let a little vent with a peg in it be made in hogshead, in some fit place above. This may be fit to broach in five or six moneths; but three weeks or a moneth before you do so, put into each hogshead half an ounce of Cinnamon; and two ounces of Cloves beaten into most subtile powder. (Sometimes he leaves out the Cloves) which will give it a most pleasant flavor; and they (as the Ginger did) sink down to the bottome and never trouble the Liquor. If they be put in long before (much more if they be boiled) they loose all their taste and Spirits entirely. This will last very well half a year drawing. But if you stay broaching it a year, and then draw it into bottles, it will keep admirable good three or four years, growing to be much better, then when broached at six months end. It will be purer, if you first boil the water by it self, then let it settle 24 hours; and pour the clear from the earthy sediment, which will be great, and dissolve your honey in that. You may Aromatise it with Ambergreece or Musk, or both (if you like them) by dissolving a very few Pastils in a Runlet of this Liquor, when you draw it into little vessels, (as He useth to do after five or six moneths) or with a few drops of the Extract of them. This Metheglin is a great Balsom and strengthener of the _Viscera_; is excellent in colds and coughs and consumptions. For which last they use to burn it (like wine) or rather onely heat it. Then dissolve the yolk of an Egge or two in a Pint of it, and some fresh Butter, and drink it warm in the morning fasting. As it comes from the Barrel or Bottle, it is used to be drunk a large draught (without any alteration or admixtion, with a toste early in the morning (eating the toste) when they intend to dine late. Consider of making Metheglin thus with purified rain water (of the _Æquinoxe_) or Dew.

The handfuls of Herbs, are natural large handfuls (as much as you can take up in your hand) not Apothecaries handfuls, which are much less.

If a pottle of Barm do not make it work enough to your mind, you may put in a little more. Discretion and Experience must regulate that.

You may make small Meathe the same way, putting but half the proportion of honey or less. But then after three weeks or a months barrelling, you must bottle it.

AN EXCELLENT WAY TO MAKE METHEGLIN, CALLED THE LIQUOR OF LIFE, WITH THESE FOLLOWING INGREDIENTS

Take Bugloss, Borage, Hyssop, Organ, Sweet-marjoram, Rosemary, French-cowslip, Coltsfoot, Thyme, Burnet, Self-heal, Sanicle a little, Betony, Blew-buttons, Harts-tongue, Meadssweet, Liverwort, Coriander two ounces, Bistort, Saint John's wort, Liquorish, Two ounces of Carraways, Two ounces of Yellow-saunders, Balm, Bugle, Half a pound of Ginger, and one ounce of Cloves, Agrimony, Tormentil-roots, Cumfrey, Fennel-root's, Clowns-all-heal, Maiden-hair, Wall-rew, Spleen-wort, Sweet-oak, Pauls-betony, Mouse ear.

For two Hogsheads of Metheglin, you take two handfuls a piece of each herb, Excepting Sanicle; of which you take but half a handful. You make it in all things as the white Meathe of Mr. Pierce's is made, excepting as followeth. For in that you boil the herbs but a quarter of an hour, that the colour may be pale: But in this, where the deepness of the colour is not regarded, you boil them a good hour, that you may get all the vertue out of them. Next for the strength of it; whereas in that, an Egge is to emerge out of the Liquor but the breadth of a three pence; in This it is to emerge a large Groats-breadth. Then in this you take but half a pound of Ginger, and one ounce of Cloves. Whereas the white hath one pound of Ginger, and two ounces of Cloves. To this you use three quarts, or rather more of Ale-yest (fresh and new) and when all your Liquor is in a high slender tall pipe with the narrowest circumference that may be (which makes it work better then a broad one, where the Spirits loose themselves) you have the yest in a large Noggin with a handle, or pail, and put some of the Liquor to it, and make that work; then pour it from pretty high unto the whole quantity in the pipe, and lade it strongly with that Noggin five or six, or eight times, pouring it every time from high, and working it well together, that so every Atome of the yest maybe mingled with every Atome of the Liquor. And this course (in this particular) you may also use in the white. It is best not to broach this, till a year be over after the making it.

TO MAKE GOOD METHEGLIN

Take to every Gallon of Honey, three Gallons of water, and put them both together, and set them over so soft a fire, that you may endure to melt and break the honey with your hands. When the honey is all melted, put in an Egge, and let it fall gently to the bottom, and if the Egge rise up to the top again of the Liquor, then is it strong enough of the honey; but if it lie at the bottom, you must put in more honey, stirring of it till it do rise. If your honey be very good, it will bear half a Gallon of water more to a Gallon of Honey. Then take Sweet-bryar, Rose-mary, Bayes, Thyme, Marjoram, Savory, of each a good handful, which must be tyed up all together in a bundle. This Proportion of herbs will be sufficient for 12 Gallons of Metheglin; and according to the quantity you make of Metheglin, you must add of your herbs or take away. When you have put these things together set it upon a quick fire, and let it boil as fast as you can for half an hour, or better, skiming of it very clean, which you must Clarifie with two or three whites of Eggs. Then take it off from the fire, and put it presently into some clean covers, and let it stand till the next morning; then pour the clear from the bottom and tun it up; putting in a little bag of such spice as you like, whereof Ginger must be the most. After it hath stood some three or four days, you may put in some two or three spoonfuls of good-ale-yest; it will make it ready the sooner to drink, if you let it work together, before you stop it up.

The older the honey is, the whiter coloured the Metheglin will be.

TO MAKE WHITE METHEGLIN OF SIR JOHN FORTESCUE

Take twelve Gallons of water, one handful of each of these herbs, Eglantine, Rosemary, Parsley, Strawberry-leaves, Wild-thyme, Balm, Liver-wort, Betony, Scabious; when your water begins to boil, cast in your herbs, and let them boil a quarter of an hour. Then strain it from the herbs. When it is almost cold, then put in as much of the best honey, as will make it bear an Egge, to the breadth of two pence; and stir it till all the honey be melted. Then boil it well half an hour at the least, and put into it the whites of six Eggs beaten to a froth to clarifie it; and when it hath drawn all the scum to the top, strain it into woodden vessels. When it is almost cold, put barm to it, and when it worketh well, Tun it into a well-seasoned vessel, where neither Ale nor Beer hath been, for marring the colour; and when it hath done working, take a good quantity of Nutmegs, Mace, Cinnamon, Cloves and Ginger bruised, and put it into a boulter bag, and hang it in the barrel.

If you will have it taste much of the spice, let it boil 3 or 4 walms in it, after you have put in the honey. But that will make it have a deep colour.

A RECEIPT FOR MEATHE

To seven quarts of water, take two quarts of honey, and mix it well together; then set it on the fire to boil, and take three or four Parsley-roots, and as many Fennel-roots, and shave them clean, and slice them, and put them into the Liquor, and boil altogether, and skim it very well all the while it is a boyling; and when there will no more scum rise, then is it boiled enough: but be careful that none of the scum do boil into it. Then take it off, and let it cool till the next day. Then put it up in a close vessel, and put thereto half a pint of new good barm, and a very few Cloves pounded and put in a Linnen-cloth, and tie it in the vessel, and stop it up close; and within a fortnight, it will be ready to drink: but if it stay longer, it will be the better.

MY LORD GORGE HIS MEATHE

Take a sufficient quantity of Rain-water, and boil in it the tops of Rose-mary, Eglantine, Betony, Strawberry-leaves, Wall-flowers, Borage and Bugloss, of each one handful; one sprig of Bays; and two or three of Sage. Then take it off the fire, and put a whole raw Egge into it, and pour so much honey to it, till the Egge rise up to the top; then boil it again, skiming it very well, and so let it cool. Then Tun it up, and put Barm to it, that it may ferment well. Then stop it up, and hang in it such spices, as you like best. It will not be right to drink under three or four moneths.

THE LADY VERNON'S WHITE METHEGLIN

Take three Gallons of water (rain water is best) boil in it broad Thyme, Rose-mary, Peny-royal, of each three handfuls. Then put it into a stone Pan to cool, and strain away the herbs; and when it is cold, put in one quart of honey, and mix it very well; then put to it one Nutmeg, a little Cinnamon; Cloves and Ginger; some Orange and Limon-peels. Then boil and scum it very well, while any scum will rise. Then put in your spices, and try with a New-laid-egg; and the stronger it is, the longer you may keep it; and if you will drink it presently, put it up in bottles, and rub the Corks with yest, that it may touch it, and it will be ready in three or four days to drink. And if you make it in the spring put no spices, but Cloves and Cinnamon, and add Violets, Cowslips, Marigolds, and Gilly-flowers; and be sure to stop your vessel close with Cork; and to this put no yest, for the Clove-gilly-flowers will set it to work.

SEVERAL SORTS OF MEATH, SMALL AND STRONG

1. SMALL. Take ten Gallons of water, and five quarts of honey, with a little Rosemary, more Sweet-bryar, some Balme, Burnet, Cloves, less Ginger, Limon Peel. Tun it with a little barm; let it remain a week in the barrel with a bag of Elder-flowers; then bottle it.

2. *Small*. Take ten quarts of water, and one of honey, Balm a little; Minth, Cloves, Limon-peel, Elder-flowers, a little Ginger; wrought with a little yest, bottle it after a night working.

3. *Strong*. Take ten Gallons of water; thirteen quarts of honey, with Angelica, Borrage and Bugloss, Rosemary, Balm and Sweet-bryar; pour it into a barrel, upon three spoonfuls of yest; hang in a bag Cloves, Elder-flowers, and a little Ginger.

4. *Very Strong*. Take ten Gallons of Water, and four of honey, with Sea-worm-wood, a little Sage, Rosemary; put it in a barrel, after three days cooling. Put no yest to it. Stop it close, and bottle it after three or

four months.

5. *Very Strong*. To ten Gallons of water take four of honey. Clarifie it with flower; and put into it Angelica, Rosemary, Bay-leaves, Balm. Barrel it without yest. Hang in a bag Cloves, Elder-flowers, a little Ginger.

6. *Very Strong*. Take ten Gallons of water, and four of Honey. Boil nothing in it. Barrel it when cold, without yest. Hang in it a bag with Cloves, Elder-flowers, a little Ginger and Limon peel; which throw away, when it hath done working, and stop it close. You may make also strong and small by putting into it Orris-roots; or with Rose-mary, Betony, Eye-bright and Wood-sorrel; or adding to it the tops of Hypericon with the flowers of it; Sweet-bryar, Lilly of the valley.

TO MAKE MEATH

Take three Gallons of water, a quart of Honey; if it be not strong enough, you may adde more. Boil it apace an hour, and scum it very clean. Then take it off, and set it a working at such heat as you set Beer, with good yest. Then put it in a Runlet, and at three days end, draw it out in stone-bottles; into everyone put a piece of Limon-peel and two Cloves. It is only put into the Runlet, whilest it worketh, to avoid the breaking of the Bottles.

SIR JOHN ARUNDEL'S WHITE MEATH

Take three Gallons of Honey, and twelve Gallons of water: mix the honey and water very well together, till the honey is dissolved; so let it stand twelve hours. Then put in a New-laid-egg; if the Liquor beareth the Egg, that you see the breadth of a groat upon the Egg dry, you may set it over the fire: if it doth not bear the Egg, then you must adde a quart or three pints more to the rest; and then set it over the fire, and let it boil gently, till you have skimed it very clean, and clarified it, as you would do Suggar, with the whites of three New-laid-eggs. When it is thus made clear from all scum, let it boil a full hour or more, till the fourth part of it is wasted; then take it off the fire; and let it stand till the next day. Then put it into a vessel. When it hath been in the barrel five or six days, make a white tost, and dip it into new yeast, and put the tost into the barrel, and let it work. When it hath done working, stop it up very close. This keep three quarters of a year. You may drink it within half a year, if you please. You may adde in the boiling, of what herbs you like the taste, or what is Physical.

TO MAKE METHEGLIN

Take eight Gallons of water, and set it over a clear fire in a Kettle; and when it is warm, put into it sixteen pounds of very good honey; stir it well together, till it be all mixed; and when it boileth, take off the scum, and put in two large Nutmegs cut into quarters, and so let it boil at least an hour. Then take it off, and put into it two good handfuls of grinded Malt, and with a white staff keep beating it together, till it be almost cold; then strain it through a hair sieve into a tub, and put to it a wine pint of Ale-yest, and stir it very well together; and when it is cold, you may, if you please, Tun it up presently in a vessel fit for it, or else let it stand, and work a day: And when it hath done working in your vessel, stop it up very close. It will be three weeks or a month, before it will be ready to drink.

TO MAKE WHITE MEATH

Take six Gallons of water, and put in six quarts of honey, stirring it till the honey be throughly melted; then set it over the fire, and when it is ready to boil, skim it very clean. Then put in a quarter of ounce of Mace, so much Ginger, half an ounce of Nutmegs, Sweet-marjoram, Broad-thyme, and Sweet-bryar, of altogether a handful; and boil them well therein; Then set it by, till it be through cold, and then Barrel it up, and keep it till it be ripe.

TO MAKE A MEATH GOOD FOR THE LIVER AND LUNGS

Take of the Roots of Coltsfoot, Fennel and Fearn each four Ounces. Of Succory-roots, Sorrel-roots, Strawberry-roots, Bitter-sweet-roots, each two Ounces, of Scabious-roots and Elecampane-roots, each an Ounce and a half. Ground-ivy, Hore-hound, Oak of Jerusalem, Lung-wort, Liver-wort, Maiden-hair, Harts-tongue of each two good-handfulls.

Licorish four Ounces. Jujubes, Raisins of the Sun and Currents, of each two Ounces; let the roots be sliced, and the herbs be broken a little with your hands; and boil all these in twenty quarts of fair running water, or, if you have it, in Rain water, with five Pints of good white honey, until one third part be boiled away; then pour the liquor through a jelly bag often upon a little Coriander-seeds, and Cinnamon; and when it runneth very clear, put it into Bottles well stopped, and set it cool for your use, and drink every morning a good draught of it, and at five in the afternoone.

TO MAKE WHITE METHEGLIN

Put to three Gallons of Spring-water, one of honey. First let it gently melt; then boil for an hour, continually skiming it; then put it into an earthen or a woodden vessel, and when it is a little more than Blood-warm, set it with Ale-yest, and so let it stand twelve hours. Then take off the yest, and bottle it up. Put into it Limon-peel and Cloves, or what best pleaseth your taste of Spice or Herbs. Eringo-roots put into it, when it is boiling, maketh it much better.

Note, That if you make Hydromel by fermentation in the hot Sun (which will last about fourty days, and requireth the greater heat) you must take it thence, before it be quite ended working; and stop it up very close, and set it in a cold Cellar, and not pierce it in two months, at the soonest. It will be very good this way, if you make it so strong, as to bear an Egge very boyant. It is best made by taking all the Canicular days into your fermentation.

A VERY GOOD MEATH

Put three parts of water to one of honey. When the Honey is dissolved, it is to bear an Egge boyant. Boil it and skim it perfectly clear. You may boil in it Pellitory of the wall, Agrimony, or what herbs you please. To every ten Gallons of water, take Ginger, Cinnamon, *ana*, one Ounce, Nutmegs half an Ounce. Divide this quantity (sliced and bruised) into two parts. Boil the one in the Meath, severing it from the Liquor, when it is boiled, by running through a strainer; and hang the other parcel in the barrel by the bung in a bag with a bullet in it. When it is cold, Tun it.

And then you may work it with barm if you please; but it is most commended without.

TO MAKE WHITE METHEGLIN

Take the Honey-combs, that the Honey is run out from them, and lay them in water over night; next day strain them, and put the Liquor a boiling; Then take the whites of two or three Eggs, and clarifie the Liquor. When you have so done, skim it clean. Then take a handful of Peny-royal; four handfuls of Angelica; a handful of Rosemary; a handful of Borrage; a handful of Maidenhair, a handful of Harts-tongue; of Liverwort, of Water-cresses, of Scurvy-grass, *ana*, a handful; of the Roots of Marshmallows, Parsley, Fennel, *ana*, one Ounce. Let all these boil together in the Liquor, the space of a quarter of an hour. Then strain the Liquor from them, and let it cool, till it be Blood-warm. Put in so much honey, until an Egge swim on it; and when your honey is melted, then put it into the Barrel. When it is almost cold, put a little Ale barm to it; And when it hath done working, put into your barrel a bag of Spice of Nutmegs, Ginger, Cloves and Mace, and grains good store; and if you will, put into a Lawn-bag two grains of Ambergreece and two grains of Musk, and fasten it in the mouth of your barrel, and so let it hang in the Liquor.

A MOST EXCELLENT METHEGLIN

Take one part of honey, to eight parts of Rain or River-water; let it boil gently together, in a fit vessel, till a third part be wasted, skiming it very well. The sign of being boiled enough is, when a New-laid-egg swims upon it. Cleanse it afterwards by letting it run through a clean Linnen-cloth, and put it into a woodden Runlet, where there hath been wine in, and hang in it a bag with Mustard-seeds by the bung, that so you may take it out, when you please. This being done, put your Runlet into the hot Sun, especially during the Dog-days, (which is the onely time to prepare it) and your Metheglin will boil like Must; after which boiling take out your Mustard-seeds, and put your vessel well stopped into a Cellar. If you will have it the taste of wine, put to thirty measures of Hydromel, one measure of the juyce of hops, and it will begin to boil without any heat. Then fill up your vessel, and presently after this ebullition you will have a very strong Metheglin.

TO MAKE WHITE METHEGLIN OF THE COUNTESS OF DORSET

Take Rosemary, Thyme, Sweet-bryar, Peny-royal, Bays, Water-cresses, Agrimony, Marshmallow leaves, Liver-wort, Maiden-hair, Betony, Eye-bright, Scabious, the bark of the Ash-tree, Eringo-roots, Green-wild-Angelica, Ribwort, Sanicle, Roman-worm-wood, Tamarisk, Mother-thyme, Sassafras, Philipendula, of each of these herbs a like proportion; or of as many of them as you please to put in. But you must put in all but four handfuls of herbs, which you must steep one night, and one day, in a little bowl of water, being close covered; the next day take another quantity of fresh water, and boil the same herbs in it, till the colour be very high; then take another quantity of water, and boil the same herbs in it, until they look green; and so let it boil three or four times in several waters, as long as the Liquor looketh any thing green. Then let it stand with these herbs in it a day and night. Remember the last water you boil it in to this proportion of herbs, must be twelve gallons of water, and when it hath stood a day and a night, with these herbs in it, after the last boiling, then strain the Liquor from the herbs, and put as much of the finest and best honey into the Liquor, as will make it bear an Egg. You must work and labour the honey and liquor together one whole day, until the honey be consumed. Then let it stand a whole night, and then let it be well laboured again, and let it stand again a clearing, and so boil it again a quarter of an hour, with the whites of six New-laid-eggs with the shells, the yolks being taken out; so scum it very clean, and let it stand a day a cooling. Then put it into a barrel, and take Cloves, Mace, Cinamon, and Nutmegs, as much as will please your taste, and beat them altogether; put them into a linnen bag, and hang it with a thread in the barrel. Take heed you put not too much spice in; a little will serve. Take the whites of two or three New-laid-eggs, a spoonful of barm, and a spoonful of Wheat-flower, and beat them altogether, and put it into your Liquor into the barrel, and let it work, before you stop it. Then afterwards stop it well, and close it well with clay and Salt tempered together, and let it be set in a close place; and when it hath been settled some six weeks, draw it into bottles, and stop it very close, and drink it not a month after: but it will keep well half a year, and more.

ANOTHER WAY TO MAKE WHITE METHEGLIN

Take ten Gallons of water; then take six handfuls of Sweet-bryar; as much of Sweet-marjoram; and as much of Muscovy. Three handfuls of the best Broad-thyme. Boil these together half an hour; then strain them. Then take two Gallons of English-honey, and dissolve it in this hot Liquor, and brew it well together; then set it over the fire to boil again, and skim it very clean; then take the whites of thirty Eggs wel beaten, and put them into the Liquor, and let it boil an hour; then strain it through a jelly bag, and let it stand 24 hours cooling: then put it up in a vessel. Then take six Nutmegs, six fair Races of Ginger, a quarter of an Ounce of Cloves, half an Ounce of Cinamon; bruise all these together, and put them into a Linnen-bag, with a little Pebble-stone to make it sink. Then hang it in the vessel. You may adde to it, if you please, two grains of Ambergreece, and one grain of Musk. Stop the vessel with a Cork, but not too close, for six days; then taste it: and if it taste enough of the Spice, then take out the bag; if not, let the bag hang in it, and stop it very close, and meddle with it no more. It will be ready to drink in nine or ten weeks.

A RECEIPT TO MAKE GOOD MEATH

Take as many Gallons of water, as you intend to make of Meath; and to every Gallon put a quart of honey, and let it boil till it bear an Egg. To every Gallon you allow the white of an Egg, which white you must remove and break with your hands, and put into the Kettle, before you put it over the fire. Before it boileth, there will arise a skum, which must be taken off very clean, as it riseth. Put to every Gallon two Nutmegs sliced, and when it hath boiled enough, take it off, and set it a cooling in clean wort-vessels: And when it is as cold as wort, put in a little barm, and work it like Beer, and when it hath done working, stop it up, and let it stand two months.

ANOTHER TO MAKE MEATH

To every quart of honey allow six Wine-quarts of water; half an Ounce of Nutmegs, and the Peel of a Limon, and the meat of two or three, as you make the quantity. Boil these together, till the scum rise no more; It must stand till it be quite cold, and when you Tun it, you squeese into it the juyce of some Limons, and this will make it ripen quickly. It will be ready in less then a month.

ANOTHER RECIPE

Take twelve Gallons of water, a handful of Muscovy (which is an herb, that smelleth like Musk), a handful of Sweet-Marjoram, and as much of Sweet-bryar. Boil all these in the water, till all the strength be out. Then take it off and strain it out, and being almost cold, sweeten it with honey very strong, more then to bear an Egg, (the meaning of this is, that when there is honey enough to bear an Egg, which will be done by one part of honey to three or four quarts of water: then you add to it a pretty deal of honey more, at least 1/4 or 1/3 of what you did put in at first to make it bear an Egg: then it is to be boiled and scummed: when it is thus strong, you may keep it four years before you drink it. But at the end of two years you may draw it out into bottles) just above it, else it will not keep very long: for the more honey the better. Then set it over the fire till it boils, and scum it very clean. Then take it from the fire, and let it stand, till it be cold: then put it into your vessel. Take Mace, Cloves, Nutmegs, Ginger, of each a quarter of an Ounce: beat them small, and hang them in your vessel (being stopped close) in a little bag.

Note, when any Meath or Metheglin grows hard or sower with keeping too long, dissolve in it a good quantity of fresh honey, to make it pleasantly Sweet; (but boil it no more, after it hath once fermented, as it did at the first Tunning) and with that it will ferment again, and become very good and pleasant and quick.

TO MAKE METHEGLIN

Take of Rosemary three handfuls, of Winter-savory a Peck by measure, Organ and Thyme, as much, White-wort two handfuls, Blood-wort half a peck, Hyssop two handfuls, Marygolds, Borage, Fennil, of each two handfuls; Straw-berries and Violet-leaves, of each one handful; Of Harts-tongue, Liverwort a peck; Ribwort half a peck, of Eglantine with the Roots, a good quantity; Wormwood as much as you can gripe in two hands; and of Sorrel, Mead-sutt Bettony with the Roots, Blew-bottles with the Roots, the like quantity; of Eye-bright two handfuls, Wood-bind one handful. Take all these herbs, and order them so, as that the hot herbs may be mastered with the cool. Then take the small herbs, and put them into the Furnace, and lay the long herbs upon them. Then take a weight or stone of Lead, having a Ring, whereunto fasten a stick to keep down the Herbs into the furnace; then boil your water and herbs three or four hours, and as the water doth boil away, adde more. Then take the water out of the Furnace seething hot, and strain it through a Range-sieve; then put in the honey, and Mash it well together: then take your Sweet-wort, and strain it through a Range. Then try it with a New-laid-egg. It must be so strong as to bear an Egg the breadth of a groat above the Liquor: and if it doth not, then put in more honey, till it will bear the Egg. Then take the Liquor, and boil it again; and as soon as it doth boil, skim the froth very clean from it: Then set it a cooling, and when it is cold, then put it into a Kive, and put barm thereto, and let it work the Space of a Week; Then Tun it up: But be careful when it is Tunned, that the vessels be not stopp'd up, till it hath done hissing.

ANOTHER SORT OF METHEGLIN

Take to one part of honey, three parts of water: and put them into clean vessels, mixing them very well together, and breaking the honey with stripped arms, till it be well dissolved. Then pour out your Liquor into a large Kettle, and let it boil for two hours and a half, over a good fire, skiming it all the while very carefully as long as any scum riseth. When it is boiled enough, pour out your Liquor into clean vessels, and set it to cool for 24 hours. Afterwards put it into some Runlets, and cover the bung with a piece of Lead: have a care to fill it up always with the same boiled Liquor for three or four months and during the time of working. This Meath the older it is, the better it is. But if you will have your Meath red, then take twenty pound of black Currants, and put them into a vessel, and pour your Liquor on them. Of this honey-Liquor you cannot drink till after nine months, or a year.

MY LORD HERBERT'S MEATH

Take ten Gallons of water; and to every Gallon of water a quart of honey, a handful and a half of Rosemary, one Ounce of Mace, one Ounce and a half of Nutmegs, as much Cinamon, half an Ounce of Cloves, a quarter of a pound of Ginger scraped and cut in pieces. Put all these into the water, and let it boil half an hour, then take it off the fire, and let it stand, till you may see your shadow in it. Then put in the honey, and set it upon the fire again. Then take the shells and whites of a dozen of Eggs, and beat them both very well together: and when it is ready to boil up, put in your Eggs, and stir it; then skim it clean, and take it off the fire, and put it into vessels to cool, as you do wort. When it is cold, set it together with some barm, as you do Beer. When it is put together leave the settlings behind in the bottom; as soon as it is white over, Tun it up in a vessel, and when it hath done working, stop it up as you do Beer. When it is three weeks old, it will be fit to bottle or drink.

ANOTHER WHITE MEATH

Take three Pound of White-honey, or the best Hampshire-honey, and dissolve it in a Gallon of water, and then boil it; and when it beginneth first to boil, put into it half a quarter of an Ounce of Ginger a little bruised; and a very little Cloves and Mace bruised, and a small quantity of Agrimony. Let all this boil together a full hour, and keep it constantly skimmed, as long as any Scum will rise upon it. Then strain it forth into some clean Kiver or other vessel, and let stand a cooling; and when it is cold, let it stand, till it be all creamed over with a blackish cream, and that it make a kind of hissing noise; then put it up into your vessel, and in two or three months time it will be fit to drink.

Look how much you intend to make, the same quantities must be allowed to every Gallon of water.

TO MAKE METHEGLIN

Take fair water, and the best honey; beat them well together, but not in a woodden vessel, for wood drinketh up the honey, put it together in a Kettle, and try it with a New-laid-egg, which will swim at top, if it be very strong; but if it bob up and sink again, it will be too weak. Boil it an hour, and put into it a bundle of herbs, what sort you like best; and a little bag of Spice, Nutmegs, Ginger, Cloves, Mace and Cinamon; and skim it well all the while it boileth: when it hath boiled an hour, take it off, and put it into earthen Pans, and so let it stand till next day. Then pour off all the clear into a good vessel, that hath had Sack in it, or White-wine. Hang the bag of Spice in it, and so let it stand very close stopp'd and well filled for a month, or longer. Then if you desire to drink it quickly, you may bottle it up. If it be strong of the honey, you may keep it a year or two. If weak, drink it in two or three months. One quart of honey, will make one Gallon of water very strong. A sprig or two of Rose-mary, Thyme and Sweet-marjoram, are the Herbs that should go into it.

TO MAKE SMALL METHEGLIN

Take to every quart of White-honey, six quarts of fair-water. Let it boil, until a third part be boiled away; skiming it as it riseth: then put into it a small quantity of Ginger largely sliced; then put it out into earthen Pans, till it be Luke-warm, and so put it up into an earthen stand, with a tap in it. Then put to it about half a Porenger-ful of the best Ale-yest, so beat it well together; Then cover it with a cloth, and it will be twelve hours before it work; and afterwards let it stand two days, and then draw it out into stone bottles, and it will be ready to drink in five or six days after. This proportion of yest (which is about six good spoonfuls) is enough for three or four Gallons of Liquor. The yest must be of good Ale, and very new. You may mingle the yest first with a little of the Luke-warm-Liquor; then beat it, till it be well incorporated, and begins to work; Then adde a little more Liquor to it, and beat that. Continue so adding the Liquor by little and little, till a good deal of it be Incorporated with the yest; then put that to all the rest of the quantity, and beat it altogether very well; then cover it close, and keep it warm for two or three days. Before you bottle it, scum away all the barm and Ginger (whereof a spoonful or two is enough for three or four Gallons) then bottle up the clear, leaving the dregs. If you will, you may Tun it into a barrel, (if you make a greater quantity) when the barm is well Incorporated with the Liquor, in the same manner as you do Beer or Ale, and so let it work in the Barrel as long as it will; then stop it up close for a few days more, that so it may clear it self well, and separate and precipitate the dregs. Then draw the clear into bottles. This will make it less windy, but also a little less quick, though more wholesome. You may also boil a little handful of tops of Rosemary in the Liquor, which giveth it a fine taste: but all other herbs, and particularly Sweet-marjoram and Thyme, give it a Physical taste. A little Limon-peel giveth it a very fine taste. If you Tun it in a barrel, to work there, you may hang the Ginger and Limon-peel in it in a bag, till you bottle it, or till it have done working. Then you may put two or three stoned and sliced Raisins, and a lump of fine Sugar into every bottle to make it quick.

TO MAKE METHEGLIN

Take five Gallons of water, and one Gallon of good White-honey; set it on the fire together, and boil it very well, and skim it very clean; Then take it off the fire, and set it by. Take six ounces of good Ginger, and two ounces of Cinamon, one Ounce of Nutmegs; bruise all these grosly, and put them into your hot Liquor, and cover it close, and so let it stand, till it be cold. Then put as much Ale-barm to it, as will make it work; then keep it in a warm place, as you do Ale; and when it hath wrought well, Tun it up, as you do Ale or Beer: and when it is a week old, drink of it at your pleasure.

AN EXCELLENT METHEGLIN

Take Spring-water, and boil it with Rose-mary, Sage, Sweet-Marjoram, Balm and Sassafras, until it hath boiled three or four hours: The quantity of the Herbs is a handful of them all, of each a like proportion, to a Gallon of water. And when it is boiled, set it to cool and to settle until the next day: Then strain your water, and mix it with honey, until it will bear an Egg the breadth of a Groat. Then set it over the fire to boil. Take the whites of twenty or thirty Eggs, and beat them mightily, and when it boileth, pour them in at twice; stir it well together, and then let it stand, until it boileth a pace before you scum it, and then scum it well. Then take it off the fire, and pour it in earthen things to cool: and when it is cold, put to it five or six spoonfuls of the best yest of Ale you can get: stir it together, and then every day scum it with a bundle of Feathers till it hath done working: Then Tun it up in a Sack-cask and to every six gallons of Metheglin put one pint of _Aquavitæ_, or a quart of Sack; and a quarter of a pound of Ginger sliced, with the Pills of two or three Limons and Orenges in a bag to hang in it.

The Whites of Eggs above named, is a fit proportion for 10 or 12 Gallons of the Liquor.

TO MAKE WHITE MEATHE

Take six Gallons of water, and put in six quarts of Honey, stirring it till the honey be throughly melted; then set it over the fire, and when it is ready to boil, skim it clean; then put in a quarter of an Ounce of Mace; so much Ginger; half an Ounce of Nutmegs; Sweet-marjoram, Broad-thyme and Sweet-Bryar, of all together a handful, and boil them well therein. Then set it by, till it be throughly cold, and barrel it up, and keep it till it be ripe.

ANOTHER TO MAKE MEATHE

To every Gallon of water, take a quart of Honey, to every five Gallons, a handful of Sweet-marjoram, half a handful of Sliced-ginger; boil all these moderately three quarters of an hour; then let it stand and cool: and being Lukewarm, put to every five Gallons, about three quarts of Yest, and let it work a night and a day. Then take off the Yest and strain it into a Runlet; and when it hath done working: then stop it up, and so let it remain a month: then drawing out into bottles, put into every bottle two or three stoned Raisins, and a lump of Loaf-sugar. It may be drunk in two months.

ANOTHER VERY GOOD WHITE MEATH

Take to every Gallon of water a quart of Honey: boil in it a little Rose-mary and Sweet-marjoram: but a large quantity of Sweet-bryar-leaves, and a reasonable proportion of Ginger: boil these in the Liquor, when it is skimed; and work it in due time with a little barm. Then tun it in a vessel; and draw it into bottles, after it is sufficiently settled. Whites of Eggs with the shells beaten together, do clarifie Meath best. If you will have your Meath cooling, use Violet and Straw-berry-leaves, Agrimony, Eglantine and the like: adding Borage and Bugloss, and a little Rosemary and Sweet-Marjoram to give it Vigor.

Tartar makes it work well.

TO MAKE WHITE METHEGLIN

Take to three Gallons of Spring-water, one of Honey; first let it gently melt, then boil for an hour, continually skiming it; then put it into an earthen or woodden vessel, and when it is little more then Blood-warm, set it with Ale-yest, and so let it stand twelve hours; then take off the Yest, and Bottle it. Put in it Limon-peel and Cloves, or what best pleaseth your taste of Herbs or Spices. Eringo-roots put into it, when it is a boiling, maketh it much better. So do Clove-gilly-flowers; a quantity of which make the Meath look like Claret-wine. I observe that Meath requireth some strong Herbs to make it quick and smart upon the Palate; as Rose-mary, Bay-leaves, Sage, Thyme, Marjoram, Winter-savory, and such like, which would be too strong and bitter in Ale or Beer.

TO MAKE WHITE MEATH

Take Rose-mary, Thyme, Sweet-bryar, Peny-royal, and Bays, Water-cresses, Agrimony, Marsh-mallows, leaves and flowers: Liver-wort, Wood-betony, Eye-bright, Scabious, of each alike quantity; of the bark of Ash-tree, of Eringo-roots-green, of each a proportion to the herbs; of wild Angelica, Ribwort, Sanicle, Roman-worm-wood, of each a proportion, which is, to every handful of the Herbs above named, a sixteenth part of a handful of these latter; steep them a night and a day, in a woodden boul of water covered; the next day boil them very well in another water, till the colour be very high; Then take another quantity of water, and boil the herbs in it, till it look green, and so let it boil three or four times, or as long as the liquor looketh any thing green;

then let it stand with these herbs in it a day and a night.

To every Gallon of this water, put a quart of pure clear honey, the Liquor being first strained from the herbs. Your Liquor if it be strong enough will bear an Egg, the breadth of a three pence above water. When you have put the honey into the Liquor, you must work and Labour it together a whole day, until the honey be consumed. Then let it stand a whole night again a clearing. Then put it into a kettle, and let it boil a quarter of an hour, with the whites and shells of six Eggs; Then strain it clean, and so let it stand a cooling. Then put it into a barrel, and take Cloves, Mace, Cinamon, Nutmegs, and beat them together: put them into a linnen bag, hang it with a thread into the barrel. If you would have it work, that you may drink of it presently, take the whites of two or three Eggs, a spoonful of barm, a spoonful of wheat-flower; beat all these together: Let it work, before you stop it up. Then afterwards stop it well with clay and salt tempered together, to keep it moist.

TO MAKE METHEGLIN

If your honey be tryed, take six Gallons of Milk-warm-water, to one of honey, and stir it well together ever and anon, and so let it stand for a day and night, or half a day may serve; then boil it with a gentle fire, for the space of half an hour or thereabouts, and skim it, still as the skum ariseth. After it is scummed once or twice, you may put in your herbs, and spice grosly beaten, one half loose; the other in a bag, which afterwards may be fastned with a string to the tap-hole, as Pepper, Cloves, Mace, Ginger and the like; when it is thus boiled, let it stand in the vessel until it be cooled; then Tun it up into your barrel, and let it work two or three days, or more before you stop the bung-hole; but in putting up the boiled liquor into the barrel, reserve the thick grounds back, which will be settled in the pan or kettle.

If you would have it to drink within two or three months, let it be no stronger then to bear an Egg to the top of the water. If you would have it keep six months, or longer, before you drink it, let it bear up the Egg the breadth of two pence above the water. This is the surer way to proportion your honey then by measure. And the time of the tryal of the strength is, when you incorporate the honey and water together, before the boiling of it.

ANOTHER SORT OF MEATH

Take thirty six Gallons of fountain water (first boiled, &c.) and dissolve twelve Gallons of Honey in it. Keep them boiling an hour and a half after they begin to boil, skimming well all the while. It will be an hour upon the fire before it boil. When it is clear and enough boiled, pour it out into woodden vessels to cool. When you are ready to Tun it, have four Gallons of Black-currants, bruise them in a stone mortar, that they may the more easily part with their juyce to the Liquor. Put them and their juyce into the barrel, and pour the cool Liquor upon them, so as the vessel be quite full. Cover the bung with a plate of lead lying loose on, that the working of the Liquor may lift it up, as it needeth to cast out the filth. And still as it worketh over, fill it up with fresh Liquor, made in the same proportion of honey and water. A moneth after it works no longer, stop up the bung very close.

TO MAKE VERY GOOD METHEGLIN

Take of all sorts of herbs, that you think are good and wholesome, as Balm, Minth, Fennel, Rosemary, Angelica, Wild-thyme, Hyssop, Agrimony, Burnet, and such other as you may like; as also some field herbs; But you must not put in too many, especially Rose-mary or any strong herb. Less then half a handfull will serve of every sort. Boil your herbs, and strain them out, and let the Liquor stand till the morrow, and settle; Then take of the clearest of the Liquor two Gallons and a half to one Gallon of Honey; and in that proportion take as much of them as you will make, and let it boil an hour, and in the boiling scum it very clean. Then set it a cooling as you do Beer; and when it is cold, take some very good Ale-barm, and put it into the bottom of the Tub you mean the Metheglin shall work in, which pour into the Tub by little and little, as they do Beer, keeping back the thick settling, which lieth in the bottome of the vessels, wherein it is cooled. And when all is put together, cover it with a cloth, and let it work very near three days. And when you mean to put it up, scum off all the barm clean, and put it up into your Barrel or Firkin, which you must not stop very close in four or five days, but let it have a little vent, for it will work; and when it is close stopped, you must look to it very often, and have a peg in the top, to give it vent, when you hear it make a noise (as it will do) or else it will break the barrel. You may also, if you please, make a bag, and put in good store of sliced Ginger, and some Cloves and Cinnamon, and boil it in, or put it into the barrel and never boil it. Both ways are good.

If you will make small Metheglin, you may put five or six Gallons of water to one of honey. Put in a little Cinnamon and Cloves and boil it well. And when it is cold, put it up in bottles very close stopped, and the stopples well tyed on. This will not keep above five or six weeks, but it is very fine drink.

Make your Metheglin as soon as ever you take your Bees; for if you wash your combs in the water you boil your herbs in, when it is cold, it will sweeten much. But you must afterwards strain it through a cloth, or else there will be much wax.

TO MAKE MEATH

If you will have it to keep a year or two, take six parts of water, and one of honey; But if you will have it to keep longer, take but four parts of water to one of honey. Dissolve the honey very well in the water, then boil it gently, skimming it all the while as the scum riseth, till no more scum riseth. Then pour it out of the Copper into a fit vessel or vessels to cool. Then Tun it up in a strong and sweet cask, and let it stand in some place, where there is some little warmth; (It will do as well without warmth, but be longer growing ripe) This will make it work. At first a course foul matter will work over; to which purpose it must be kept always full with fresh Liquor of the same, as it worketh over. When it begins to work more gently, and that which riseth at the top, is no more foul, but is a white froth; then fill and stop it up close, and set it in a cool cellar, where it is to stand continually.

After half a year or a year, you may draw it off from the Lees into a clean vessel, or let it remain untouched. It is not fit to be drunk for it's perfection till the sweetness be quite worn off, yet not to be sower, but vinous. You may drink it at meals instead of wine, and is wholesomer and better then wine.

To small Meath, that is to be drunk presently, you may put a little Ginger to give it life, and work it with a little barm. If the Meath work not at all, it will nevertheless be good, and peradventure better than that which worketh; but it will be longer first, and the dregs will fall down to the bottom, though it work not.

Small Meath of eight or nine parts of water to one of honey, will be very good, though it never work, but be barrell'd up as soon as it is cold, and stopped close: and after two or three months drunk from the barrel without botteling. This is good for Meals.

TO MAKE WHITE MEATH

Take to every three Gallons of water, one Gallon of honey and set the water over the fire, and let the honey melt, before the water be too hot; then put in a New-laid-egg, and feel with your hand; if it comes half way the water, it is strong enough; Then put into it these Herbs, Thyme, Sweet-marjoram, Winter-savoury, Sweet-bryar, and Bay-leaves, in all a good great handful; which a proportion for ten Gallons; Then with a quick-fire boil it very fast half an hour, and no longer; and then take it from the fire, and let it cool in two or three woodden vessels; and let it stand without stirring twenty four hours. Then softly drain it out, leaving all the dregs behind. Put the clear into your vessel; and if you like any spice, take Ginger, Nutmeg, Cinnamon, Mace and Cloves, and bruise them a little, and put them in a bag, and let them hang in your vessel. Before you put your Meath into the vessel, try if it will bear an Egg as broad as a peny; if it do, then it is very well; and if it be made with the best White-honey, it usually is just so. But if it should prove too strong, that it bears the Egge broader; then boil a little more honey and water very small, and put to it, when it is cold: and then put it into the vessel. It is best to be made at Michaelmas, and not drunk of till Lent.

TO MAKE SMALL WHITE MEATH

Take of the best white honey six quarts; of Springwater sixteen Gallons;

set it on a gentle fire at first, tell it is melted, and clean skimmed; then make it boil apace, until the third part be consumed. Then take it from the fire, and put it in a cooler, and when it is cold, Tun it up, and let it stand eight months, before you drink it. When you take it from the fire, slice in three Orris-roots, and let it remain in the Liquor, when you Tun it up.

A RECEIPT TO MAKE METHEGLIN

Take four Gallons of water, two quarts of Honey, two ounces of Ginger, one ounce of Nutmegs, a good handful of Rose-mary tops, and as much of Bay-leaves, two ounces of dried Orange-peel. Boil all these till it be so strong as will bear an Egg, and not sink; when it is milk warm, work it up with barm, during twenty four hours, and then barrel it up. And after three months you may bottle it up at your pleasure.

As you desire a greater quantity of the drink, you must augment the ingredients, according to the proportions above recited.

TO MAKE METHEGLIN

Take four Gallons of water and one of Honey; boil and skim it: then put into it, Liverwort, Harts-tongue, Wild-carrot, and Yarrow, a little Rosemary and Bays, one Parsly-root, and a Fennel-root; let them boil an hour altogether. You may, if you please, hang a little bag of spice in it. When it is cold, put a little barm to it, and let it work like Beer. The roots must be scraped, and the Pith taken out.

MEATH FROM THE MUSCOVIAN AMBASSADOUR'S STEWARD

Take three times as much water as honey; then let the tubs, that the honey must be wrought in, be cleansed very clean with scalding water, so that it may not prove sowre; also when you mix them together, take half-warm-water, and half cold, and squeese them well together; Afterwards when you think the honey is well melted, then let it run through a sieve; and see your kettle of Copper or Iron (but Copper is better than Iron) be very clean; then put in your spice, as, Nutmegs,

Ginger, Cloves, Cardamome, Anisseeds, Orange peel; put these in according to the quantity you make, and let them all be bruised, except the Orange peel, which leave whole. The Meath must boil an hour by the Clock; after put it into Tubs to cool, and when it is cold, take three or four slices of White-bread, tost them very hard, and spread very good yest on both sides of the tosts; then put them into the Tubs. If it be warm weather, let the Tubs be uncovered; but if it be cold, cover them. This being done, you will find it worked enough by the black that cometh up by the sides of the Tubs; then take a sieve and take off the yest and bread. Afterwards draw it off at a tap in the Tub into the cask you intend to keep it in; then take a quantity of spice as before, well-bruised, and put it into a bag, and make it fast at the bung, with a string, and if it begins to work, after it is in the cask, be sure to give it vent, or else you will loose all.

TO MAKE MEATH

To every quart of honey put four quarts of Springwater; temper the honey in the water, being a little warmed; then put it on the fire again, with Fennel, Rose-mary, Thyme, Agrimony, Parsley or the like. Let them boil half an hour, and upwards; and as it boileth, scum the froth; Then take it off, and strain it, and let it cool as you do your wort. Then put a little barm into it, then take off the froath again, and stir it well together. Then take two quarts of Ale, boiled with Cloves. Mace, Cinnamon, Ginger and Liquorice; and put it to the Meath and Tun it up.

A RECEIPT TO MAKE WHITE MEATH

Take Rose-mary, Thyme, Sweet-bryar, Peny-royal, Bays, Water-cresses, Agrimony, Marsh-mallow-leaves and flowers, Liver-wort, Maiden-hair, Betony, Eye-bright, Scabious, the bark of an Ash-tree, young Eringo-roots, Wild-Angelica, Ribwort, Sinacle, Roman-worm-wood, Tamarisk, Mother-thyme, Saxafrage, Philipendula, of each of these herbs a like proportion; or of as many as you please to put in. You must put in all but four handfuls of herbs, which you must steep a night and a day, in a little bowl of water, being close covered. The next day take another fresh quantity of water, and boil the same herbs in it, till the colour be very high; then take another quantity of water, and boil the same herbs in it, untill it look green; and so let them boil three or four times in several waters, as long as the Liquor looketh anything green. Then let it stand with these herbs in it a day and a night. Remember the last water you boil it in, to this proportion of herbs, must be eighteen Gallons. And when it hath stood a day and a night with these herbs in it after the last boiling, then strain the Liquor from the herbs; and put as much of the finest and best honey into the Liquor, as will bear an Egg; you must work the honey and liquor together a whole day, until the honey be consumed; then let it stand one whole night; then let it be well laboured again, and set it a clearing; and so boil it again with the whites of six New-laid-eggs with the shells; skim it very clean; and let it stand a day a cooling; then put it into a barrel, and take Cloves, Mace, Cinnamon and Nutmegs as much as will please your taste, and beat them all together, and put them in a Linnen bag, and hang it with a thread into the barrel. Then take the whites of two or three New-laid-eggs, a spoonful of barm, a spoonful of Wheat-flower, and beat them all together, and put it into your Liquor in the barrel, and let it work before you stop it; then afterwards stop it well, and set it in a cold place, and when it hath been settled some six weeks: draw it into bottles, and stop it very close, and drink not of it in a month after.

TO MAKE METHEGLIN

Take eight Gallons of water, set it over a clear fire in a Kettle; and when it is warm, put it to sixteen pounds of very good honey, and stir it well together; take off the scum, and put two large Nutmegs cut in quarters, and so let it boil at least an hour; Then take it off the fire, and put to it two good handfulls of grinded Malt, and with a white staff keep beating it together till it be almost cold; then strain it through a hair-sieve into a Tub, and put to it a wine-pint of Ale-yest, and stir it very well together; and when it is cold, you may if you please, Tun it up presently into a vessel fit for it, or else let it stand, and work a day, and when it hath done working in your vessel, stop it up very close. It will be three weeks or a month before it be ready to drink.

TO MAKE HONEY DRINK

To two quarts of water take one pound of Honey. When it boileth, skim it clean as long as any scum ariseth; boil it a pretty while; then take it off the fire, and put it in an earthen pot, and let it stand till the next day; then put it into clean bottles, that are throughly dry, rinsing first every bottle with a little of the liquor; Fill them not too full, and put into every bottle four or five Cloves, and four or five slices of Ginger: and stop it very close, and set it in Sand; and within ten or twelve days it will be ready to drink.

Some, when they take their Bees, put the honey-combs into fair-water, and make it so strong of the honey that it will bear an Egg; and then boil it with some Spice, and put it into a barrel: but I think it not so good, as that which is made of pure honey.

THE EARL OF DENBIGH'S METHEGLIN

Take twenty Gallons of Spring-water; boil it a quarter of an hour, and let it stand, until it be all most cold; then beat in so much honey, as will make it so strong as to bear an Egg, so that on the Top, you may see the breadth of a hasel-nut swimming above; The next day boil it up with six small handfuls of Rosemary; a pound and a half of Ginger, being scraped and bruised; then take the whites of twenty Eggs shells and all; beat them very well, and put them in to clarifie it; skim it very clean, then take it off the fire and strain: But put the Rosemary and Ginger in again: then let it remain till it be all most cold: then Tun it up, and take some New-ale-yest; the whites of two Eggs, a spoonful of flower, and beat them well together, and put them into the barrel; when it hath wrought very well, stop it very close for three weeks or a month: then bottle it, and a week after you may drink it.

TO MAKE MEATH

Take to every Gallon of water, a quart of honey, and set it over a clear fire, and when it is ready to boil, skim it very clear. Then take two handfulls of Sweet-marjoram, as much Rose-mary, and as much Baulm: and two handful of Fennel-roots, as much of Parsley-roots, and as many Esparages-roots: slice them in the middle, and take out the pith, wash and scrape them very clean, and put them with your herbs into your Liquor. Then take two Ounces of Ginger, one Ounce of Nutmegs, half an Ounce of Mace: bruise them and put them in: and let it boil till it be so strong that it will bear an Egg: then let it cool: and being cold, put in 3 or 4 spoon fulls of New-ale yest: and so skim it well, and put it into a Runlet, and it will work like Ale: and having done working, stop it up close, as you do New-beer: and lay salt upon it.

TO MAKE METHEGLIN

Take four Gallons of running water, and boil it a quarter of an hour, and put it in an earthen vessel, and let it stand all night. The next day take only the water, and leave the settling at the bottom: so put the honey in a thin bag, and work it in the water, till all the honey is dissolved. Take to four Gallons of water, one Gallon of Honey: Then put in an Egg, if it be strong enough of the honey, the Egg will part of it appear on the top of the liquor: if it do not, put more honey to it, till it do. Then take out the Egg, and let the Liquor stand till next morning. Then take two Ounces of Ginger, and slice it and pare it: Some Rose-mary washed and stripped from the stalk: dry it very well. The next day put the Rose-mary and Ginger into the drink, and so set it on the fire: when it is all most ready to boil, take the whites of three Eggs well beaten with the shells, and put all into the Liquor: and stir it about, and skim it well till it be clear. Be sure you skim not off the Rose-mary and Ginger: then take it off the fire, and let it run through a hair sieve: and when you have strained it, pick out the Rose-mary and Ginger out of the strainer, and put it into the drink, and throw away the Eggshells, and so let it stand all night. The next day Tun it up in a barrel: Be sure the barrel be not too big: then take a little flower and a little bran, and the white of an Egg, and beat them well together, and put them into the barrel on the top of the Metheglin, after it is tunned up, and so let it stand till it hath done working; then stop it up as close as is possible: and so let it stand six or seven weeks: then draw it out and bottle it. You must tye down the Corks, and set the bottles in sand five or six weeks, and then drink it.

ANOTHER MEATH

Take twenty Gallons of fair Spring-water. Boil it a quarter of an hour, then let it stand till the next day. Then beat into it so much honey, as will make it so strong as to bear an Egg the breadth of a two pence above the water. The next day boil it up with six small handfulls of Rosemary, a pound and a half of Ginger, (being scraped and bruised) and the whites of twenty Eggs together with their shells beaten together, and well mingled with the Liquor. Clarifie it and skim it very clean, still as the scum riseth, leaving the Ginger and Rosemary in it. Let it stand till the next day, then Tun it up, and take some New-ale-yest, the whites of two Eggs, a spoonful of flower, beat all these together, and put it on the top of the barrel, when the barrel is full. Let it work, and when it hath done working, stop it up close for three weeks, or a month. Then you may bottle it, and a few days after, you may drink it.

ANOTHER

Take three Gallons of water, and boil in it a handful of Rose-mary (or rather the flowers) Cowslips, Sage-flowers, Agrimony, Betony, and Thyme, *ana*, one handful. When it hath taken the strength of the herbs, strain it through a hair-sieve, and let it cool twenty hours. Then to three Gallons of the clear part of this decoction, put one Gallon of honey, and mingle it very well with your hand, till it bear an Egg the breadth of a groat. Then boil it and skim it as long as any scum will rise. Afterwards let it cool twenty four hours. Then put to it a small quantity of Ale-barm, and skim the thin-barm that doth rise on it, morning and evening, with a feather, during four days. And so put it up into your vessel, and hang in it a thin linnen bag with two Ounces of good White-ginger bruised therein: And stop it up close for a quarter of a year. Then you may drink it.

ANOTHER

Take a quart of honey to a Gallon of water; set the Kettle over the fire, and stir it now and then, that the honey may melt; let it boil an hour; you must boil in it, a Sprig or two of Winter-savory, as much of Sweet-marjoram; put it into tubs ready scalded, till the next day towards evening. Then tun it up into your vessel, let it work for three days; after which hang a bag in the barrel with what quantity of Mace and sliced Nutmeg you please. To make it stronger then this, 'tis but adding more hony, to make it bear an Egg the breadth of a six pence, or something more. You may bottle it out after a month, when you please. This is the way, which is used in Sussex by those who are accounted to make it best.

ANOTHER RECEIPT

Take to every Gallon of Fountain-water a good quart of honey. Set the water on the fire, till it be pretty warm; then take it off, and put it in your honey, and stir it till it be dissolved. Then put into every three Gallons, two handfuls of Thyme: two good handfuls of Strawberry-leaves, one handful of Organ; one handful of Fennel-roots, the heart being taken out, and one handful of Parsley-roots the heart taken out: But as for the herbs, it must be according to the constitution of them, for whom the Mead is intended. Then set the Herbs in it on the fire, to boil for half an hour, still skimming it, as the scum riseth; it must boil but half an hour; then take it off the fire, and presently strain it from the herbs, and let it stand till it be fully cold; then pour it softly off the bottom, and put it in a vessel fit for it, and put a small quantity of barm in it, and mingle it with it, and when it hath wrought up, which will be in three or four days, skim off that barm, and set on fresh: but the second barm must not be mingled with the Meath, but onely poured on the top of it. Take an Ounce of Nutmeg sliced: one Ounce of Ginger sliced: one Ounce of Cinnamon cut in pieces, and boil them a pretty while in a quart of White-wine or Sack: when this is very cold, strain it, and put the spices in a Canvas-bag to hang in your Meath, and pour in the Wine it was boiled in.

This Meath will be drinkable, when it is a fortnight or three weeks old.

TO MAKE METHEGLIN THAT LOOKS LIKE WHITE-WINE

Take to twelve gallons of water, a handful of each of these Herbs: Parsley, Eglantine, Rosemary, Strawberry-leaves, Wild-thyme, Baulme, Liverwort, Betony, Scabious: when the water begins to boil, cast in the herbs: let them boil a quarter of an hour: then strain out the herbs; and when it is almost cold, then put in as much of the best honey, you can get, as will bear an Egg to the breadth of two pence; that is, till you can see no more of the Egge above the water, then a two pence will cover:

Lave it and stir it till you see all the honey be melted; then boil it well half an hour, at the least: skim it well, and put in the whites of six Eggs beaten, to clarifie it: Then strain it into some woodden vessels; and when it is almost cold, put some Ale-barm into it. And when it worketh well, Tun it into some well seasoned vessel, where neither Ale nor Beer hath been, for marring the colour of it. When it hath done working, if you like it, Take a quantity of Cloves, Nutmegs, Mace, Cinnamon, Ginger, or any of these that you like best, and bruise them, and put them in a boulter bag, and hang it in the vessel. Put not too much of the Spice, because many do not like the taste of much Spice. If you make it at Michaelmas, you may tap it at Christmas: but if you keep it longer, it will be the better. It will look pure, and drink with as much spirit as can be, and very pleasant.

TO MAKE WHITE METHEGLIN

Take Sweet-marjoram, Sweet-bryar-buds, Violet-leaves, Strawberry-leaves, of each one handful, and a good handful of Violet flowers (the dubble ones are the best) broad Thyme, Borrage, Agrimony, of each half a handful, and two or three branches of Rosemary, The seeds of Carvi, Coriander, and Fennel, of each two spoonfuls, and three or four blades of large-mace. Boil all these in eight Gallons of running-water, three quarters of an hour. Then strain it, and when it is but blood-warm, put in as much of the best honey, as will make the Liquor bear an Egg the breadth of six pence above the water. Then boil it again as long as any scum will rise. Then set it abroad a cooling; and when it is almost cold, put in half a pint of good Ale-barm; and when it hath wrought, till you perceive the barm to fall, then Tun it, and let it work in the barrel, till the barm leaveth rising, filling it up every day with some of the same Liquor. When you stop it up, put in a bag with one Nutmeg sliced, a little whole Cloves and Mace, a stick of Cinnamon broken in pieces, and a grain of good Musk. You may make this a little before Michaelmas, and it will be fit to drink at Lent.

This is Sir Edward Bainton's Receipt, Which my Lord of Portland (who gave it me) saith, was the best he ever drunk.

TO MAKE A SMALL METHEGLIN

Take four Gallons of water, and set it over the fire. Put into it, when it is warm, eight pounds of honey; as the scum riseth, take it clean off. When it is clear, put into it three Nutmegs quartered; three or four Races of Ginger sliced; Then let it boil a whole hour, Then take it off the fire, and put to it two handfuls of ground Malt; stir it about with a round stick, till it be as cold as wort, when you put yest to it. Then strain it out into a pot or Tub, that hath a spiggot and faucet, and put to it a pint of very good Ale-yest; so let it work for two days; Then cover it close for about four or five days, and so draw it out into bottles. It will be ready to drink within three weeks.

TO MAKE MEATH

Take to six quarts of water, a quart of the best honey, and put it on the fire, and stir it, till the honey is melted: and boil it well as long as any scum riseth: and now and then put in a little cold water, for this will make the scum rise: keep your kettle up as full as you did put it on; when it is boiled enough, about half an hour before you take it off, then take a quantity of Ginger sliced and well scraped first, and a good quantity of Rosemary, and boil both together. Of the Rosemary and Ginger you may put in more or less, for to please your taste: And when you take it off the fire, strain it into your vessel, either a well seasoned-tub, or a great cream pot, and the next morning when it is cold, pour off softly the top from the settlings into another vessel; and then put some little quantity of the best Ale-barm to it and cover it with a thin cloth over it, if it be in summer, but in the winter it will be longer a ripening, and therefore must be the warmer covered in a close place, and when you go to bottle it, take with a feather all the barm off, and put it into your bottles, and stop it up close. In ten days you may drink it.

If you think six quarts of water be too much, and would have it stronger, then put in a greater quantity of honey.

METHEGLIN OR SWEET DRINK OF MY LADY STUART

Take as much water as will fill your Firkin: of Rosemary, Bays, Sweet-bryar, Broad-thyme, Sweet-majoram, of each a handful; set it over the fire, until the herbs have a little coloured the water; then take it off, and when it is cold, put in as much honey, till it will bear an Egg; Then lave it three days morning and evening. After that boil it again, and skim it very clean, and in the boiling clarifie it with the whites of six Eggs, shells and all, well beaten together. Then take it off, and put it to cool; and when it is cold, put it into your vessel, and put to it three spoonfuls of yest; stop it close, and keep it, till it be old at least three months.

A METHEGLIN FOR THE COLICK AND STONE OF THE SAME LADY

Take one Gallon of Honey to seven Gallons of water; boil it together, and skim it well; then take Pelitory of the Wall, Saxifrage, Betony, Parsley, Groundsel, of each a handful, of the seeds of Parsley, of Nettles, Fennel and Carraway-seeds, Anisseeds and Grumelseeds, of each two Ounces. The roots of Parsley, of Alexander, of Fennel and Mallows of each two Ounces, being small cut; let all boil, till near three Gallons of the Liquor is wasted: Then take it off the fire, and let it stand till it be cold; then cleanse it from the drugs, and let it be put into a clean vessel well stopped, taking four Nutmegs, one Ounce and half of Ginger, half an Ounce of Cinnamon, twelve Cloves; cut all these small, and hang them in a bag into the vessel, when you stop it up. When it is a fortnight old, you may begin to drink of it; every morning a good draught.

A RECEIPT FOR METHEGLIN OF MY LADY WINDEBANKE

Take four Gallons of water; add to it, these Herbs and Spices following. Pellitory of the Wall, Sage, Thyme, of each a quarter of a handful, as much Clove gilly-flowers, with half as much Borage and Bugloss flowers, a little Hyssop, Five or six Eringo-roots, three or four Parsley-roots: one Fennel-root, the pith taken out, a few Red-nettle-roots, and a little Harts-tongue. Boil these Roots and Herbs half an hour; Then take out the Roots and Herbs, and put in the Spices grosly beaten in a Canvass-bag, _viz._ Cloves, Mace, of each half an Ounce, and as much Cinnamon, of Nutmeg an Ounce, with two Ounces of Ginger, and a Gallon of Honey: boil all these together half an hour longer, but do not skim it at all: let it boil in, and set it a cooling after you have taken it off the fire. When it is cold, put six spoonfuls of barm to it, and let it work twelve hours at least; then Tun it, and put a little Limon-peel into it: and then you may bottle it, if you please.

ANOTHER OF THE SAME LADY

To four Gallons of water put one Gallon of honey; warm the water Luke-warm before you put in your honey; when it is dissolved, set it over the fire, and let it boil half an hour with these Spices grosly beaten and put in a Canvass-bag: namely, half an Ounce of Ginger, two Nutmegs, a few Cloves and a little Mace; and in the boiling put in a quart of cold water to raise the scum, which you must take clean off in the boiling. If you love herbs, put in a little bundle of Rosemary, Bays, Sweet-marjoram and Eglantine. Let it stand till it is cold, then put into it half a pint of Ale-barm, and let it work twelve hours; then Tun it, but take out the bundle of herbs first.

TO MAKE METHEGLIN

Take to every Gallon of Honey, three Gallons of water, and put them together and set them over so gentle a fire, as you might endure to break it in the water with your hand. When the Honey is all melted, put in an Egg, and let it fall gently to the bottom; and if your Egg rise up again to the top of the Liquor, then it is strong enough of the Honey. But if it lie at the bottom, you must put in more honey, and stir it, till it doth rise. If your honey be very good, it will bear half a Gallon of water more to a Gallon of Honey. Then take Sweet-bryar, Bays, Rosemary, Thyme, Marjoram, Savoury, of each a good handfull, which you must tye up all together in a bundle. This Proportion of Herbs will be sufficient for twelve Gallons of Metheglin; and according to the quantity of Metheglin you make, you must add or diminish your Herbs. When you have put these things together, set it over a quick fire, and let it boil as fast as you can for half an hour or better, skiming of it very clean and clarifying it with the whites of two or three Eggs. Then take it from the fire, and put it into some clean vessel or other, and let it stand till the next morning; Then pour the Clear from the dregs, and Tun it up, putting in a little bag of such Spice as you like, whereof

Ginger must be the most. After it hath stood three or four days, you may put in two or three spoon-fulls of good Ale-yest, it will make it the sooner ready to drink. It must work before you stop it up. The older your Honey is, the whiter your Metheglin will be.

MEATH WITH RAISINS

Put forty Gallons of water into your Caldron, and with a stick take the height of the water, making a notch, where the superficies of the water cometh. Then put to the water ten Gallons of Honey, which dissolve with much Laving it; then presently boil it gently, skimming it all the while, till it be free from scum. Then put into it a thin bag of boulter-cloth containing forty pound weight of the best blew Raisins of the Sun, well picked and washed and wiped dry; and let the bag be so large, that the Raisins may lie at ease and loosly in it. When you perceive that the Raisins are boiled enough to be very soft, that you may strain out all their substance, take out the bag, and strain out all the Liquor by a strong Press. Put it back to the Honey-liquor, and boil all together (having thrown away the husks of the Raisins with the bag) till your Liquor be sunk down to the notch of your stick, which is the sign of due strength. Then let it cool in a woodden vessel, and let it run through a strainer to sever it from the settlings, and put it into a strong vessel, that hath had Sack or Muscadine in it, not filling it to within three fingers breadth of the top (for otherwise it will break the vessel with working) and leave the bung open whiles it worketh, which will be six weeks very strongly, though it be put into a cold cellar. And after nine moneths, you may begin to drink it.

MORELLO WINE

To half an Aume of white wine, take twenty pounds of Morello Cherries, the stalks being first plucked off. Bruise the Cherries and break the stones. Pour into the Wine the juyce that comes out from the Cherries; but put all the solid substance of them into a long bag of boulter-cloth, and hang it in the Wine at the bung, so that it lie not in the bottom, but only reach to touch it, and therefore nail it down at the mouth of the bung. Then stop it close. For variety, you may put some clear juyce of Cherries alone (but drawn from a larger proportion of

Cherries) into another parcel of Wine. To either of them, if you will Aromatise the drink, take to this quantity two Ounces of Cinnamon grosly broken and bruised, and put it in a little bag at the spiggot, that all the wine you draw may run through the Cinnamon.

You must be careful in bruising the Cherries, and breaking the stones. For if you do all at once, the Liquor will sparkle about. But you must first bruise the Cherries gently in a mortar, and rub through a sieve all that will pass, and strain the Residue hard through your hands. Then beat the remaining hard so strongly, as may break all the stones. Then put all together, and strain the clean through a subtil strainer, and put the solider substance into the bag to hang in the Wine.

CURRANTS-WINE

Take a pound of the best Currants clean picked, and pour upon them in a deep straight mouthed earthen vessel six pounds or pints of hot water, in which you have dissolved three spoonfuls of the purest and newest Ale-yest. Stop it very close till it ferment, then give such vent as is necessary, and keep it warm for about three days, it will work and ferment. Taste it after two days, to see if it be grown to your liking. As soon as you find it so, let it run through a strainer, to leave behind all the exhausted currants and the yest, and so bottle it up. It will be exceeding quick and pleasant, and is admirable good to cool the Liver, and cleanse the blood. It will be ready to drink in five or six days after it is bottled; And you may drink safely large draughts of it.

SCOTCH ALE FROM MY LADY HOLMBEY

The Excellent Scotch Ale is made thus. Heat Spring-water; it must not boil, but be ready to boil, which you will know by leaping up in bubbles. Then pour it to the Malt; but by little and little, stirring them strongly together all the while they are mingling. When all the water is in, it must be so proportioned that it be very thick. Then cover the vessel well with a thick Mat made on purpose with a hole for the stick, and that with Coverlets and Blankets to keep in all the heat. After three or four hours, let it run out by the stick (putting new heated water upon the Malt, if you please, for small Ale or Beer) into a Hogshead with the head out. There let it stand till it begin to blink, and grow long like thin Syrup. If you let it stay too long, and grow too thick, it will be sowre. Then put it again into the Caldron, and boil it an hour or an hour and a half. Then put it into a Woodden-vessel to cool, which will require near forty hours for a hogshead. Then pour it off gently from the settling. This quantity (of a hogshead) will require better then a quart of the best Ale-barm, which you must put to it thus. Put it to about three quarts of wort, and stir it, to make it work well. When the barm is risen quick scum it off to put to the rest of the wort by degrees. The remaining Liquor (that is the three quarts) will have drawn into it all the heavy dregs of the barm, and you may put it to the Ale of the second running, but not to this. Put the barm, you have scummed off (which will be at least a quart) to about two gallons of the wort, and stir it to make that rise and work. Then put two Gallons more to it. Doing thus at several times, till all be mingled, which will require a whole day to do. Cover it close, and let it work, till it be at it's height, and begin to fall, which may require ten or twelve hours, or more. Watch this well, least it sink too much, for then it will be dead. Then scum off the thickest part of the barm, and run your Ale into the hogshead, leaving all the bung open a day or two. Then lay a strong Paper upon it, to keep the clay from falling in, that you must then lay upon it, in which you must make a little hole to let it work out. You must have some of the same Liquor to fill it up, as it works over. When it hath done working, stop it up very close, and keep it in a very cold Cellar. It will be fit to broach after a year; and be very clear and sweet and pleasant, and will continue a year longer drawing; and the last glass full be as pure and as quick as the first. You begin to broach it high. Let your Cask have served for Sweet-wine.

TO MAKE ALE DRINK QUICK

When small Ale hath wrought sufficiently, draw into bottles; but first put into every bottle twelve good raisins of the Sun split and stoned; Then stop up the bottle close, and set it in sand (gravel) or a cold dry Cellar. After a while this will drink exceeding quick and pleasant. Likewise take six Wheat-corns, and bruise them, and put into a bottle of Ale; it will make it exceeding quick and stronger.

TO MAKE CIDER

Take a Peck of Apples, and slice them, and boil them in a barrel of water, till the third part be wasted; Then cool your water as you do for wort, and when it is cold, you must pour the water upon three measures of grown Apples. Then draw forth the water at a tap three or four times a day, for three days together. Then press out the Liquor, and Tun it up; when it hath done working, then stop it up close.

A VERY PLEASANT DRINK OF APPLES

Take about fifty Pippins; quarter and core them, without paring them: for the paring is the Cordialest part of them. Therefore onely wipe or wash them well, and pick away the black excrescence at the top; and be sure to leave out all the seeds, which are hot. You may cut them (after all the superfluities are taken away) into thinner slices, if you please. Put three Gallons of Fountain water to them in a great Pipkin, and let them boil, till the Apples become clear and transparent; which is a sign, they are perfectly tender, and will be in a good half hour, or a little more. Then with your Ladle break them into Mash and Pulpe, incorporated with the water; letting all boil half an hour longer, that the water may draw into it self all the vertue of the Apples. Then put to them a pound and a half of pure dubble refined Sugar in powder, which will soon dissolve in that hot Liquor. Then pour it into an Hippocras bag, and let it run through it two or three times, to be very clear. Then put it up into bottles; and after a little time, it will be a most pleasant, quick, cooling, smoothing drink. Excellent in sharp Gonorrhoeas.

SIR PAUL NEALE'S WAY OF MAKING CIDER

The best Apples make the best Cider, as Pearmains, Pippins, Golden-pippins, and the like. Codlings make the finest Cider of all. They must be ripe, when you make Cider of them: and is in prime in the Summer season, when no other Cider is good. But lasteth not long, not beyond Autumn. The foundation of making perfect Cyder consisteth in not having it work much, scarce ever at all; but at least, no second time; which Ordinary Cider doth often, upon change of weather, and upon motion: and upon every working it grows harder. Do then thus:

Choose good Apples. Red streaks are the best for Cider to keep; Ginet-moils the next, then Pippins. Let them lie about three weeks, after they are gathered; Then stamp and strain them in the Ordinary way, into a woodden fat that hath a spigot three or four fingers breadth above the bottom. Cover the fat with some hair or sackcloth, to secure it from any thing to fall in, and to keep in some of the Spirits, so to preserve it from dying; but not so much as to make it ferment. When the juyce hath been there twelve hours, draw it by the spigot (the fat inclining that way, as if it were a little tilted) into a barrel; which must not be full by about two fingers. Leave the bung open for the Air to come in, upon a superficies, all along the barrel, to hinder it from fermenting; but not so large a superficies as to endanger dying, by the airs depredating too many spirits from it.

The drift in both these settlings is, that the grosser parts consisting of the substance of the Apple, may settle to the bottom, and be severed from the Liquor; for it is that, which maketh it work again (upon motion or change of weather) and spoils it. After twenty four hours draw of it, to see if it be clear, by the settling of all dregs, above which your spigot must be. If it be not clear enough, draw it from the thick dregs into another vessel, and let it settle there twenty four hours. This vessel must be less then the first, because you draw not all out of the first. If then it should not be clear enough, draw it into a third, yet lesser than the second; but usually it is at the first. When it is clear enough draw it into bottles, filling them within two fingers, which stop close. After two or three days visit them; that if there be a danger of their working (which would break the bottles) you may take out the stopples, and let them stand open for half a quarter of an hour. Then stop them close, and they are secure for ever after. In cold freesing weather, set them upon Hay, and cover them over with Hay or Straw. In open weather in Winter transpose them to another part of the Cellar to stand upon the bare ground or pavement. In hot weather set them in sand. The Cider of the Apples of the last season, as Pippins, not Peermains, nor codlings, will last till the Summer grow hot. Though this never work, 'tis not of the Nature of Strummed Wine; because the naughty dregs are not left in it.

DOCTOR HARVEY'S PLEASANT WATER-CIDER, WHEREOF HE USED TO DRINK MUCH, MAKING IT HIS ORDINARY DRINK

Take one Bushel of Pippins, cut them into slices with the Parings and Cores; boil them in twelve Gallons of water, till the goodness of them be in the water; and that consumed about three Gallons. Then put it into an Hypocras-bag, made of Cotton; and when it is clear run out, and almost cold, sweeten it with five pound of Brown-sugar, and put a pint of Ale-yest to it, and set it a working two nights and days: Then skim off the yest clean, and put it into bottles, and let it stand two or three days, till the yest fall dead at the top: Then take it off clean with a knife, and fill it up a little within the neck (that is to say, that a little about a fingers breadth of the neck be empty, between the superficies of the Liquor, and the bottom of the stopple) and then stop them up and tye them, or else it will drive out the Corks. Within a fortnight you may drink of it. It will keep five or six weeks.

ALE WITH HONEY

Sir Thomas Gower makes his pleasant and wholesom drink of Ale and Honey thus. Take fourty Gallons of small Ale, and five Gallons of Honey. When the Ale is ready to Tun, and is still warm, take out ten Gallons of it; which, whiles it is hot, mingle with it the five Gallons of Honey, stirring it exceeding well with a clean arm till they be perfectly incorporated. Then cover it, and let it cool and stand still. At the same time you begin to dissolve the honey in this parcel, you take the other of thirty Gallons also warm, and Tun it up with barm, and put it into a vessel capable to hold all the whole quantity of Ale and Honey, and let it work there; and because the vessel will be so far from being full, that the gross foulness of the Ale cannot work over, make holes in the sides of the Barrel even with the superficies of the Liquor in it, out of which the gross feculence may purge; and these holes must be fast shut, when you put in the rest of the Ale with the Honey: which you must do, when you see the strong working of the other is over; and that it works but gently, which may be after two or three or four days, according to the warmth of the season. You must warm your solution of honey, when you put it in, to be as warm as Ale, when you Tun it; and then it will set the whole a working a fresh, and casting out more foulness; which it would do too violently, if you put it in at the first of the Tunning it. It is not amiss that some feculence lie thick upon the Ale, and work not all out; for that will keep in the spirits. After you have dissolved the honey in the Ale, you must boil it a little to skim it; but skim it not, till it have stood a while from the fire to cool; else you will skim away much of the Honey, which will still rise as long as it boileth. If you will not make so great a quantity at a time, do it in less in the same proportions. He makes it about Michaelmas for Lent.

When strong Beer groweth too hard, and flat for want of Spirits, take four or five Gallons of it out of a Hogshead, and boil five pounds of honey in it, and skim it, and put it warm into the Beer; and after it hath done working, stop it up close. This will make it quick, pleasant and stronger.

SMALL ALE FOR THE STONE

The Ale, that I used to drink constantly of, was made in these proportions. Take fourteen Gallons of Water, and half an Ounce of Hops; boil them near an hour together. Then pour it upon a peck of Malt. Have a care the Malt be not too small ground; for then it will never make clear Ale. Let it soak so near two hours. Then let it run from the Malt, and boil it only one walm or two. Let it stand cooling till it be cool enough to work with barm, which let be of Beer rather than Ale, about half a pint.

After it hath wrought some hours, when you see it come to it's height, and is near beginning to fall in working, Tun it into a barrel of eight Gallons; and in four or five days it will be fit to broach to drink. Since I have caused the wort to be boiled a good half hour; since again I boil it a good hour, and it is much the better; because the former Ale tasted a little Raw. Now because it consumes in boiling, and would be too strong, if this Malt made a less proportion of Ale; I have added a Gallon of water at the first, taking fifteen Gallons instead of fourteen. Since I have added half a peck of Malt to the former proportions, to make it a little stronger in Winter.

APPLE DRINK WITH SUGAR, HONEY, &c

A very pleasant drink is made of Apples, thus; Boil sliced Apples in water, to make the water strong of Apples, as when you make to drink it for coolness and pleasure. Sweeten it with Sugar to your tast, such a quantity of sliced Apples, as would make so much water strong enough of Apples; and then bottle it up close for three or four months. There will come a thick mother at the top, which being taken off, all the rest will be very clear, and quick and pleasant to the taste, beyond any Cider. It will be the better to most taste, if you put a very little Rosemary into the liquor, when you boil it, and a little Limon-peel into each bottle, when you bottle it up.

TO MAKE STEPPONI

Take a Gallon of Conduit-water, one pound of blew Raisins of the Sun stoned, and half a pound of Sugar. Squeese the juyce of two Limons upon the Raisins and Sugar, and slice the rindes upon them. Boil the water, and pour it so hot upon the ingredients in an earthen pot, and stir them well together. So let it stand twenty four hours. Then put it into bottles (having first let it run through a strainer) and set them in a Cellar or other cool place.

WEAK HONEY-DRINK

Take nine pints of warm fountain water, and dissolve in it one pint of pure White-honey, by laving it therein, till it be dissolved. Then boil it gently, skimming it all the while, till all the scum be perfectly scummed off; and after that boil it a little longer, peradventure a quarter of an hour. In all it will require two or three hours boiling, so that at last one third part may be consumed. About a quarter of an hour before you cease boiling, and take it from the fire, put to it a little spoonful of cleansed and sliced Ginger; and almost half as much of the thin yellow rinde of Orange, when you are even ready to take it from the fire, so as the Orange boil only one walm in it. Then pour it into a well-glased strong deep great Gally-pot, and let it stand so, till it be almost cold, that it be scarce Luke-warm. Then put to it a little silver-spoonful of pure Ale-yest, and work it together with a Ladle to make it ferment: as soon as it beginneth to do so, cover it close with a fit cover, and put a thick dubbled woollen cloth about it. Cast all things so that this may be done when you are going to bed. Next morning when you rise, you will find the barm gathered all together in the middle; scum it clean off with a silver-spoon and a feather, and bottle up the Liquor, stopping it very close. It will be ready to drink in two or three days; but it will keep well a month or two. It will be from the first very quick and pleasant.

MR. WEBB'S ALE AND BRAGOT

Five Bushels of Malt will make two Hogsheads. The first running makes one very good Hogshead, but not very strong; the second is very weak. To this proportion boil a quarter of a Pound of Hops in all the water that is to make the two Hogsheads; that is, two Ounces to each Hogshead. You put your water to the Malt in the Ordinary way. Boil it well, when you come to work it with yest, take very good Beer-yest, not Ale-yest.

To make Bragot, He takes the first running of such Ale, and boils a less proportion of Honey in it, then when He makes His ordinary Meath; but dubble or triple as much spice and herbs. As for Example to twenty Gallons of the Strong-wort, he puts eight or ten pound, (according as your taste liketh more or less honey) of honey; But at least triple as much herbs, and triple as much spice as would serve such a quantity of small Mead as He made Me (For to a stronger Mead you put a greater proportion of Herbs and Spice, then to a small; by reason that you must keep it a longer time before you drink it; and the length of time mellows and tames the taste of the herbs and spice). And when it is tunned in the vessel (after working with the barm) you hang in it a bag with bruised spices (rather more then you boiled in it) which is to hang in the barrel all the while you draw it.

He makes also Mead with the second weak running of the Ale; and to this He useth the same proportions of honey, herbs and spice, as for his small Mead of pure water; and useth the same manner of boiling, working with yest, and other Circumstances, as in making of that.

THE COUNTESS OF NEWPORT'S CHERRY WINE

Pick the best Cherries free from rotten, and pick the stalk from them; put them into an earthen Pan. Bruise them, by griping and straining them in your hands, and let them stand all night; on the next day strain them out (through a Napkin; which if it be a course and thin one, let the juyce run through a Hippocras or gelly bag, upon a pound of fine pure Sugar in powder, to every Gallon of juyce) and to every gallon put a pound of Sugar, and put it into a vessel. Be sure your vessel be full, or your wine will be spoiled; you must let it stand a month before you bottle it; and in every bottle you must put a lump (a piece as big as a Nutmeg) of Sugar. The vessel must not be stopt until it hath done working.

STRAWBERRY WINE

Bruise the Strawberries, and put them into a Linnen-bag which hath been a little used, that so the Liquor may run through more easily. You hang in the bag at the bung into the vessel, before you do put in your Strawberries. The quantity of the fruit is left to your discretion; for you will judge to be there enough of them, when the colour of the wine is high enough. During the working, you leave the bung open. The working being over, you stop your vessel. Cherry-wine is made after the same fashion. But it is a little more troublesome to break the Cherry-stones. But it is necessary, that if your Cherries be of the black soure Cherries, you put to it a little Cinnamon, and a few Cloves.

TO MAKE WINE OF CHERRIES ALONE

Take one hundred pounds weight, or what quantity you please, of ripe, but sound, pure, dry and well gathered Cherries. Bruise and mash them with your hands to press out all their juyce, which strain through a boulter cloth, into a deep narrow Woodden tub, and cover it close with clothes. It will begin to work and ferment within three or four hours, and a thick foul scum will rise to the top. Skim it off as it riseth to any good head, and presently cover it again. Do this till no more great quantity of scum arise, which will be four or five times, or more. And by this means the Liquor will become clear, all the gross muddy parts rising up in scum to the top. When you find that the height of the working is past, and that it begins to go less, tun it into a barrel, letting it run again through a boulter, to keep out all the gross feculent substance. If you should let it stay before you tun it up, till the working were too much deaded, the wine would prove dead. Let it remain in the barrel close stopped, a month or five weeks. Then draw it into bottles, into each of which put a lump of fine Sugar, before you draw the wine into it, and stop them very close, and set them in a cold Cellar. You may drink them after three or four months. This wine is exceeding pleasant, strong, spiritful and comfortable.

OF COOKERY

TO MAKE A SACK POSSET

Boil two wine-quarts of Sweet-cream in a Possnet; when it hath boiled a little, take it from the fire, and beat the yolks of nine or ten fresh Eggs, and the whites of four with it, beginning with two or three spoonfuls, and adding more till all be incorporated; then set it over the fire, to recover a good degree of heat, but not so much as to boil; and always stir it one way, least you break the consistence. In the mean time, let half a pint of Sack or White muscadin boil a very little in a bason, upon a Chafing-dish of Coals, with three quarters of a pound of Sugar, and three or four quartered Nutmegs, and as many pretty big pieces of sticks of Cinnamon. When this is well scummed, and still very hot, take it from the fire, and immediately pour into it the cream, beginning to pour neer it, but raising by degrees your hand so that it may fall down from a good height; and without anymore to be done, it will then be fit to eat. It is very good kept cold as well as eaten hot. It doth very well with it, to put into the Sack (immediately before you put in the cream) some Ambergreece, or Ambered-sugar, or Pastils. When it is made, you may put powder of Cinnamon and Sugar upon it, if you like it.

ANOTHER

To two quarts of Cream, if it be in the Summer, when the Cream is thick and best, take but two or three yolks of Eggs. But in the Winter when it is thin and hungry, take six or seven; but never no whites. And of Sack or Muscadin, take a good third (scarce half) of a pint; and three quarters of a pound of fine Sugar. Let the Sugar and Sack boil well together, that it be almost like a Syrup; and just as you take it from the fire, put in your ground Amber or Pastils, and constantly pour in the Cream with which the Eggs are incorporated; and do all the rest as is said in the foregoing Process.

Ambered-sugar is made by grinding very well, four grains of Ambergreece, and one of Musk, with a little fine Sugar; or grinding two or three Spanish Pastils very small.

A PLAIN ORDINARY POSSET

Put a pint of good Milk to boil; as soon as it doth so, take it from the fire, to let the great heat of it cool a little; for doing so, the curd will be the tenderer, and the whole of a more uniform consistence. When it is prettily cooled, pour it into your pot, wherein is about two spoonfuls of Sack, and about four of Ale, with sufficient Sugar dissolved in them. So let it stand a while near the fire, till you eat it.

A SACK POSSET

Take three pints of Cream; boil in it a little Cinnamon, a Nutmeg quartered, and two spoonfuls of grated bread; then beat the yolks of twelve Eggs very well with a little cold Cream, and a spoonful of Sack. When your Cream hath boiled about a quarter of an hour, thicken it up with the Eggs, and sweeten it with Sugar; and take half a pint of Sack and six spoonfuls of Ale, and put into the basin or dish, you intend to make it in, with a little Ambergreece, if you please. Then pour your Cream and Eggs into it, holding your hand as high as conveniently you can, gently stirring in the basin with the spoon as you pour it; so serve it up. If you please you may strew Sugar upon it.

You may strew Ambred sugar upon it, as you eat it; or Sugar-beaten with Cinnamon, if you like it.

A BARLEY SACK POSSET

Take half a pound or more of French barley, (not Perle-barley) and pour scalding water upon it, and wash it well therein, and strain it from the water, & put it into the Corner of a Linnen-cloth and tie it up fast there, and strike it a dozen or twenty blows against a firm table or block, to make it tender by such bruising it, as in the Countrey is used with wheat to make frumenty. Then put it into a large skillet with three pints of good milk. Boil this till at least half be consumed, and that it become as thick as hasty pudding, which will require at least two hours; and it must be carefully stirred all the while, least it burn too: which if by some little inadvertence it should do, and that some black burned substance sticketh to the bottom of the skillet, pour all the good matter from it into a fresh skillet (or into a basin whiles you scoure this) and renew boiling till it be very thick; All which is to make the barley very tender and pulpy, and will at least require two or near three hours. Then pour to it three pints of good Cream, and boil them together a little while, stirring them always. It will be sometime before the cold Cream boil, which when it doth, a little will suffice. Then take it from the fire, and season it well with Sugar. Then take a quarter of a pint of Sack, and as much Rhenish-wine (or more of each) and a little Verjuyce, or sharp Cider, or juyce of Orange, and season it well with Sugar (at least half a pound to both) and set it over Coals to boil. Which when it doth, and the Sugar is well melted, pour the Cream into it; in which Cream the barley will be settled to the bottom by standing still unmoved, after the Sugar is well stirred and melted in it, or pour it through a hair-sieve; and you may boil it again, that it be very hot, when you mingle them together; else it may chance not curdle. Some of the barley (but little) will go over with it, and will do no hurt. After you have thus made your Posset, let it stand warm a while that the curd may thicken: but take heed it boil not, for that would dissolve it again into the consistence of Cream. When you serve it up, strew it over with Powder of Cinnamon and Sugar. It will be much the better, if you strew upon it some Ambergreece ground with Sugar. You may boil bruised sticks of Cinnamon in the Cream, and in the Sack, before you mingle them. You must use clear Char-coal-fire under your vessels. The remaining barley will make good barley Cream, being boiled with fresh Cream and a little Cinnamon and Mace; to which you may add a little Rosemary and Sugar, when it is taken from the fire: or butter it as you do wheat. Or make a pudding of it, putting to it a Pint of Cream, which boil; then add four or five yolks, and two whites of Eggs, and the Marrow of two bones cut small, and of one in lumps: sufficient Sugar, and one Nutmeg grated. Put this either to bake raw, or with puff-past beneath and above it in the dish. A pretty smart heat, as for white Manchet, and three quarters of an hour in the Oven. You may make the like with great Oat-meal scalded (not boiled) in Cream, and soaked a night; then made up as the other.

MY LORD OF CARLILE'S SACK-POSSET

Take a Pottle of Cream, and boil in it a little whole Cinnamon, and three or four flakes of Mace. To this proportion of Cream put in eighteen yolks of Eggs, and eight of the whites; a pint of Sack; beat your Eggs very well, and then mingle them with your Sack. Put in three quarters of a pound of Sugar into the Wine and Eggs with a Nutmeg grated, and a little beaten Cinnamon; set the basin on the fire with the wine and Eggs, and let it be hot. Then put in the Cream boyling from the fire, pour it on high, but stir it not; cover it with a dish, and when it is settled, strew on the top a little fine Sugar mingled with three grains of Ambergreece, and one grain of Musk, and serve it up.

A SYLLABUB

My Lady Middlesex makes Syllabubs for little Glasses with spouts, thus. Take 3 pints of sweet Cream, one of quick white wine (or Rhenish), and a good wine glassful (better the 1/4 of a pint) of Sack: mingle with them about three quarters of a pound of fine Sugar in Powder. Beat all these together with a whisk, till all appeareth converted into froth. Then pour it into your little Syllabub-glasses, and let them stand all night. The next day the Curd will be thick and firm above, and the drink clear under it. I conceive it may do well, to put into each glass (when you pour the liquor into it) a sprig of Rosemary a little bruised, or a little Limon-peel, or some such thing to quicken the taste; or use Amber-sugar, or spirit of Cinnamon, or of Lignum-Cassiæ; or Nutmegs, or Mace, or Cloves, a very little.

A GOOD DISH OF CREAM

Boil a quart of good Cream with sticks of Cinnamon and quartered Nutmeg and Sugar to your taste. When it is boiled enough to have acquired the taste of the Spice, take the whites of six New laid eggs, and beat them very well with a little Fresh-cream, then pour them to your boyling Cream, and let them boil a walm or two. Then let it run through a boulter, and put a little Orange flower-water to it, and sliced bread; and so serve it up cold.

AN EXCELLENT SPANISH CREAM

Take two quarts (you must not exceed this proportion in one vessel) of perfectly Sweet-cream, that hath not been jogged with carriage; and in a Possnet set it upon a clear lighted Char-coal-fire, not too hot. When it beginneth to boil, cast into it a piece of double refined hard Sugar about as much as two Walnuts, and with a spoon stir the Cream all one way. After two or three rounds, you will perceive a thick Cream rise at the top. Scum it off with your spoon, and lay it in another dish. And always stir it the same way, and more Cream will rise; which as it doth rise, you put it into your dish, one lare upon an other. And thus almost all the Cream will turn into this thick Cream, to within two or three spoonfuls. If you would have it sweeter, you may strew some Sugar upon the top of it. You must be careful not to have the heat too much; for then it will turn to oyl; as also if the Cream have been carried. If you would have it warm, set the dish you lay it in, upon a Chafing-dish of Coals.

ANOTHER CLOUTED CREAM

Milk your Cows in the evening about the ordinary hour, and fill with it a little Kettle about three quarters full, so that there may be happily two or three Gallons of Milk. Let this stand thus five or six hours. About twelve a Clock at night kindle a good fire of Charcoal, and set a large Trivet over it. When the fire is very clear and quick, and free from all smoak, set your Kettle of Milk over it upon the Trivet, and have in a pot by a quart of good Cream ready to put in at the due time; which must be, when you see the Milk begin to boil simpringly. Then pour in the Cream in a little stream and low, upon a place, where you see the milk simper: This will presently deaden the boiling, and then you must pour in no more Cream there, but in a fresh place, where it simpreth and bubbeleth a little. Continue this pouring in, in new places where the milk boileth, till all your Cream is in, watching it carefully to that end. Then let it continue upon the fire to boil, till you see all the Milk rise up together to the top, and not in little parcels here and there, so that it would run over, if it should stay longer upon the fire. Then let two persons take it steadily off, and set it by in a Cool-room to stand unmoved, uncovered; but so as no Motes may fall in, for the rest of that night, and all the next day and night, and more, if you would have it thicker. Then an hour or two before Dinner cut the thick Cream at the top with a Knife into squares as broad as your hand, which will be the thicker the longer it hath stood. Then have a thin slice or skimmer of Latton, and with that raise up the thick Cream, putting your slice under it so nicely, that you take up no milk with it; and have a Ladle or Spoon in the other hand to help the cream upon the slice, which thereby will become mingled: and lay these parcels of Cream in a dish, into which you have first put a little raw Cream, or of that (between Cream and Milk) that is immediately under the Clouts. To take the Clouts the more conveniently, you hold a back of a Ladle or skimming-dish against the further side of the Clout, that it may not slide away when the Latton slice shuffeth it on the other side to get under it, and so the Clout will mingle together or dubble up, which makes it the thicker, and the more graceful. When you have laid a good Laire of Clouts in the dish, put upon it a little more fresh raw or boiled cream, and then fill it up with the rest of the Clouts. And when it is ready to serve in, you may strew a little Sugar upon it, if you will you may sprinkle in a little Sugar between every flake or clout of Cream. If you keep the dish thus laid a day longer before you eat it, the Cream will grow the thicker and firmer. But if you keep it, I think it is best to be without sugar or raw Cream in it, and put them in, when you are to serve it up. There will be a thin Cream swimming upon the milk of the Kettle after the Clouts are taken away, which is very sweet and pleasant to drink. If you should let your clouts lie longer upon the milk, then I have said, before you skim it off, the Milk underneath would grow soure, and spoil the cream above. If you put these clouts into a Churn with other cream, it will make very good butter, so as no sugar have been put with it.

MY LORD OF S. ALBAN'S CRESME FOUETTEE

Put as much as you please to make, of sweet thick cream into a dish, and whip it with a bundle of white hard rushes, (of such as they make whisks to brush cloaks) tyed together, till it come to be very thick, and near a buttery substance. If you whip it too long, it will become butter. About a good hour will serve in winter. In summer it will require an hour and a half. Do not put in the dish, you will serve it up in, till it be almost time to set it upon the table. Then strew some poudered fine sugar in the bottom of the dish it is to go in, and with a broad spatule lay your cream upon it: when half is laid in, strew some more fine sugar upon it, and then lay in the rest of the Cream (leaving behinde some whey that will be in the bottom) and strew more sugar upon that. You should have the sugar-box by you, to strew on sugar from time to time, as you eat off the superficies, that is strewed over with sugar. If you would have your whipped cream light and frothy, that hath but little substance in the eating, make it of onely plain milk; and if you would have it of a consistence between both, mingle cream and milk.

TO MAKE THE CREAM CURDS

Strain your Whey, and set it on the fire; make a clear and gentle fire under your kettle; as they rise, put in Whey, so continuing till they are ready to skim. Then take your skimmer, and put them on the bottom of a hair sieve, so let them drain till they are cold; then take them off, and put them into a basin, and beat them with two or three spoonfuls of Cream and Sugar.

TO MAKE CLOUTED CREAM

Take two Gallons more or less of new milk, set it upon a clear fire; when it is ready to boil, put in a quart of sweet cream, and take it off the fire, and strain it through a hair sieve into earthen pans; let it stand two days and two nights; then take it off with a skimmer; strew sugar on the cream, and serve it to the Table.

END

www.ingramcontent.com/pod-product-compliance
Lightning Source LLC
Chambersburg PA
CBHW081123080526
44587CB00021B/3723